THE OXFORD UNION
GUIDE TO SPEAKING
IN PUBLIC

This book will help you to:
Build confidence through special exercises and games
Understand how your listeners think
Learn how to argue logically, analytically and effectively
Discover the secrets of 'spinning' your speech to the media

Also includes:
Special chapters on business meetings and weddings
Some of the greatest speeches in history

D1635193

THE OXFORD UNION GUIDE TO SPEAKING IN PUBLIC

Dr Dominic Hughes and
Benedict Phillips

To our families

This edition first published in Great Britain in 2004 by
Virgin Books Ltd
Thames Wharf Studios
Rainville Road
London W6 9HA

First published as *The Oxford Union Guide to Successful Public Speaking*
in 2000 by Virgin Publishing Ltd

ISBN 0 7535 0955 5

Typeset by TW Typesetting, Plymouth, Devon
Printed and bound in Great Britain by
Clays Ltd, St Ives PLC

CONTENTS

ACKNOWLEDGEMENTS

This is the first time in its 177-year history that the Oxford Union has gone into print in this manner. There are many people who have made this possible. We are particularly grateful to the following for their help and support:

Natalie Acton, Kirstie Addis, Lucy Aitkens, Geeta Bandi-Phillips, Jeff Bell, Stella Burch, David Bussey, Georgina Costa, Helen Eastman, Dr Rowan Finch, Thomas Goodhead, Jeremy Hoare, Roger Houghton, Christopher Hughes, Gail Hughes, Marcus, Christian and Emma Hughes, Sally Hughes, Rachael Jukes, Dr Kostas Kalogerakis, Dr Vanita Kara, Chris Keane, Anna Kirk, Stacey Kriel, Robert Lands, Rev'd James Leach, Dr Peter Lunn, Rachel Manolson, Linda McPhee, Joshua Meggitt, Helyn Mensah, Dr Simone Murray, Dan Neidle, Oxford Union DSC, Peggy Pao Pei Yu, Christopher and Clare Phillips, Katherine Phillips, Nick Phillips, Humphrey Price, Amanda Pritchard, Jesse Rosenthal, Ben Seifert, Dr John Stevenson, Erico Tanaka, Edward Tomlinson, Stephen Twigg MP, Dr Ellie Wainwright, Christopher Walton, Lindsey Warne, Dr Ben White, Wragge and Co. Solicitors.

This is by no means a comprehensive list of all those to whom we owe a debt of thanks. We have benefited greatly from the feedback of students, colleagues and friends in India, Japan, the Netherlands, South Africa, the UK and the USA. We are very grateful to them all.

DWH · BJHP
Oxford – London – The Hague, 5 January 2000

We are also very grateful to the following parties for their permission to reproduce previously published material: John O'Farrell, Stephen Fry and Hugh Laurie, Jane Fonda, Lou Gehrig, Jonathan Lynn, Antony Jay and BBC Worldwide Limited, George Mikes and Penguin Books Ltd, Robert Reich, Oliver Thomson, Rt Hon. David Trimble MP and Gough Whitlam AC QC.

INTRODUCTION

1. ANYONE CAN BE A GREAT PUBLIC SPEAKER

'Raw energy', 'fresh', 'menacingly talented'. The use of clichéd expressions of awe has become something of a ritual that seems to follow great presentations, speeches or lectures. But why are such expressions heard so frequently? In part it is because many of us undervalue our *own* ability to speak well. The self-doubts and worries that all of us have about public speaking are, however, usually unfounded. Everyone, in our experience, has the ability to give a great speech: public speakers, like magicians, need no special powers.

BE YOURSELF

You don't need to adopt a lofty and statesmanlike style to be a great speaker. You just need to be yourself. Thus, Chris Patten, former Governor of Hong Kong, noted the very different speaking styles that have worked for great political leaders:

> Watch President Clinton work a room or a crowd, admire the intellectual thuggishness of Dennis Healey . . . and watch Margaret Thatcher slaughter and pillage her way through a meeting, teasing some curious half-baked statistic in a footnote to the official paper under discussion into the rhetorical equivalent of Semtex.[1]

None of those leaders succeeded by trying to be one of the others. *Learning* from each other is very different from *copying* each other. The latter is a risky option – often because the role models we choose to copy are television or film characters, rather than real people. These are probably the very worst role models of all. For example, countless fictional courtroom dramas have drummed into us a strong image of how good lawyers behave: they are very sharp, very young and invariably have a father who used to be a lawyer – 'one of the best'. They pace the courtroom, shout 'objection' and win cases through a sort of reckless freethinking that endears them to a judge who says at the end, 'You know what, kid? You're all right.' However, were any real lawyers to adopt such a persona, the best possible result would be pity from the judge and jail for the client. The great speakers we seek to copy often only exist on the screen.

Sometimes the role models we copy *are* real, but even then imitation is unlikely to lead to success. When town councillors discussing bus timetables try to sound like Winston Churchill preparing the nation to take on an implacable enemy, they don't end up sounding like Churchill at all; they just sound ridiculous. So too do the caricatured Shakespearean 'ack-tor', the fake Cockney, and the jargon-spouting pseudo-intellectual.

THROW AWAY THE RULEBOOK

Great speakers are not, then, made by pretending to be other people. Nor are they made by obeying simplistic formulae. Too much instruction in public speaking has focussed on arbitrary and unexplained rules that confuse the uninitiated and are uniformly broken by the experienced. This style of public speaking instruction stretches right back to ancient times, when Aristotle (in his *Rhetoric*) decreed that only 'elderly men' should use maxims or proverbs in their speeches. Since then, public speaking theorists have created an unhelpful and bewildering array of immutable laws of speech. Among the most bizarre of these are a set of rigid hand gestures that Abraham Fraunce decided should accompany certain types of speech. Fraunce's laws of hand gestures insisted absolutely that 'there is no gesture of the left hand alone', even though common sense may dictate otherwise.

In the aftermath of World War II, enormous sums of money were directed into researching the way people are influenced and persuaded by speech and propaganda. It was hoped that a scientific set of 'rules of persuasion' could be found. However, very few general patterns emerged from the work. The way messages are received appears to depend on a whole host of interdependent factors such as the previous experiences of the speaker and the listener, the content of the speech, the style of the speech and so on. Public speaking, it seems, cannot be boiled down to a scientific formula.

We don't believe in issuing commandments from on high. We believe that a speech should reflect something of the character of the speaker, in the same way that a conversation reflects the personalities of the participants. The aim of this book is to 'free up' speakers, so as to enable them to deliver a great speech in their own style.

THE AUDIENCE IS THE ONLY JUDGE

If there are no 'Great Men' to copy or 'commandments' to follow, how should we judge a speech? By its effect on the audience. They are the only judges. Public speaking is a uniquely 'democratic' (cynics would say 'demagogic') form of expression. A play or a poem or a painting can be great even if it attracts few, repulses many and bores most people. A speech that provokes confusion, repulsion or boredom in the audience, however, must be judged a failure. To say that *the audience* has failed is to echo Bertold Brecht's joke about the old East German Government needing to oust the public and elect a better one.

A great speech will influence the audience in the manner that you want. If speaking at a protest rally, you might want to *inspire* your audience. If speaking in a debate, you might want to *persuade* your audience. If speaking at a wedding, you might want to *entertain* your audience. Great speaking is goal-oriented.

The best initial feedback you can get from an audience member about your speech is not, therefore, 'Hey, you're a great public speaker.' If that *is* the first thing that everybody says to you after you have given a speech, it does not automatically mean that all is well. It seems to have a 'but' behind it. If you have spoken effectively, the first thing that should come in to the minds of the listeners is not that you are a great public speaker but that they *agree* with you. If, sitting on a jury, the first thought that came into your mind when hearing the defence counsel was that she was a 'good lawyer', would that make you more sympathetic to her arguments? Or more suspicious? Wouldn't the lawyer have done a better job if instead your first thought had been that she had made a *compelling case*?

Looking like a smooth speaker does not always help you to influence the audience. You won't win an argument with an angry husband or wife if you look like you are trying to stylishly manoeuvre them, dazzle them and outsmart them with rhetoric. Great speakers, like all persuasive people, don't convey the impression of being showmen. That doesn't mean an end to rhetoric; it means that rhetoric develops from personal style. As was once said of two speakers of old: 'When Cicero spoke, they said, "What a great speech." When Demosthenes spoke, they said, "Let's march." '[2]

2. WHY THIS IS NOT JUST ANOTHER PUBLIC SPEAKING BOOK

In this book, we discuss several topics that many traditional public speaking guides miss out. One such concept is the 'Intellectual Outlaw' – a simple technique that great political speakers often use to make their speeches seem more controversial (and therefore more exciting). Attempts to *sound* controversial often end in failure. Take, for example, the MP who, when recently interviewed by David Frost, insisted that 'there *should* be less war and more peace' – a novel policy which presumably out-manoeuvred the opposition. You can add controversy and radicalism to your speech in a much more elegant way than this, and on page 30, we'll show you how.

We also take a look at how the words you use can be vital in conveying the right impression. Why is it, for example, that

Finance Ministers who 'spend' money are always less popular than those who 'invest' money? Why do 'youths' mug people, whereas 'young people' just have problems? And how *do* international peace brokers arrive at 'the right form of words' when settling disputes? The answer to all these questions lies on pages 89 to 109, where we study the effects of language on your speech.

Another topic unique to this book is a rigorous analysis of why some arguments are stronger than others. Consider, for example, the following observation on life in Britain's Parliament: 'It's a wonderful place to take friends to lunch – although it should have a snooker table – and you always end up sitting next to someone interesting.'[3] What is it, exactly, that makes such comments sound so intellectually lightweight? To fully appreciate the flaws in such statements (and the weightiness in others), we'll take a detailed look at some elements of logic – such as contradictions, analogies and the use of evidence – that are important to the intellectual rigour of an argument.

Presentation is another key issue. Although often dismissed as merely an 'add-on' to the substance of the speech, it is actually of central importance. Good presentation is not just concerned with the speaker, but with the look of the *whole scene*. The great film director Orson Welles, for example, believed that the audience should be able to understand the relationships between the actors in a scene purely by noting where they were standing and who they were standing with. The image, in other words, tells us as much as the script. Drawing on Welles' advice, as well as that of psychologists, advertisers and even propaganda merchants, we'll discuss how to ensure that your speech creates the right overall image.

As well as dealing with the subtleties of public speaking, this book is also packed full of practical hints for speakers, such as the best times of day to speak, how to use hi-tech audio-visual aids and how to use specialist voice techniques to build rapport with others. Three case studies deal with the extra skills speakers need for media appearances, business meetings and wedding speeches.

In the final section, we look at some of the greatest speeches ever made, and show that great public speaking is not the preserve of politicians from eighteenth-century Britain or Ancient Greece, for excellence can be found whenever the principles of audience-centred speaking are followed. What magic ingredient, for example, made the style of argument used in a speech by Sojourner Truth, a former slave, so great that we can still learn from it almost 150 years later? What can a baseball player teach us about speech construction? And why have generations of American Presidents tried to emulate the style of Abraham Lincoln's Gettysburg Address?

In summary, public speaking is not about rules or role models, but how to change people's minds. This book will help you to win over even the most hostile audiences in *every* type of situation, from arguments over the kitchen table to speeches broadcast on television.

THE BASICS

THE BASICS OF SPEECH-BUILDING

Many public speaking guides read as if they are written only to analyse speech rather than to help make people better speakers. They often begin with the first categories of *analysis*, rather than with the most important things a speaker should know *now*. In doing so they make the same mistake as the language teacher who starts with grammar tables rather than with 'hello', 'how are you?' and 'thank you'. We have decided therefore, as Ella Fitzgerald might have sung, to 'begin at the begin'. More experienced speakers may want to go straight to later chapters, in particular the ones on content (page 53 onwards) and language (from page 89). Even the best speakers, however, may want to remind themselves of the key principles of effective public speaking, the pillars on which all else rests. In which case, start here . . .

1. SHOULD YOU SPEAK?
It can be very flattering to be asked to give a speech. There are, however, many occasions when you should think seriously before accepting an invitation to speak. All publicity is not always good publicity. Thus, public speaking instructor Robert Anholt advises would-be conference speakers that 'the decision *not* to speak is sometimes more beneficial to a person's reputation than a speech devoid of data'.[1]

If you're invited to address an audience, the first thing to consider is whether the invitation allows you to achieve your goals. Do you want to unveil a new idea or a new strategy? If so, decide if now is the best time. Do you want your speech to draw attention to a cause you feel strongly about? Then consider whether it is likely to be unfavourably edited by broadcasters and reporters. Do you want to change people's minds? Then decide whether your audience will be too hostile or volatile to listen properly.

None of these good reasons for considering declining an invitation to speak, however, should lend any support to the more common reason for doing so – fear of public speaking. As we have said, no one is incapable of public speaking. At the same time, 'difficult' public speaking experiences are unavoidable steps on the way to becoming a great speaker.

2. SPEECH MATERIAL

Contrary to popular belief, great ideas do not come about by adopting a bowed head and a pensive, contemplative look (see Rodin's *The Thinker*), nor do they come when gently reclining with a clove cigarette. As artistic as such images are, the sad reality is that most people have their best thoughts in the bath, or just before they fall asleep, or when staring aimlessly at posters on train platforms. We've all experienced that feeling when a thought suddenly just pops into our head, be it a design for a new invention, a great plan for work, or just an unusual idea for a present. The Kikuyu people of East Africa even give such sudden, insightful thoughts a special name: *Meciria*.[2]

As far as public speaking is concerned, such ideas are the key to writing a good speech. Don't rush to write your speech immediately after accepting an invitation to speak. Instead, mull things over. If, during idle moments, you think of a good point to make (or, for wedding speeches, a good story occurs to you about the bride and groom) then write it down and file it. A few days before your speech, you'll find that you've collected lots of these scraps of paper, and there are plenty of ideas and points to make. Most of the greatest speeches were written like this. Lincoln didn't finalise his great Gettysburg Address on paper until the morning of the ceremony, but reworked it many times in his head.[3]

There is another benefit to letting your speech grow like this. Many people find, for example, that after buying a car they suddenly notice lots of people driving the same model. Lots of people were, of course, always driving the same model – but your brain knows that you find your new car interesting, so it alerts you if it sees another one. In exactly the same way, if you let your speech evolve in the back of your mind, your brain will alert you when it sees something interesting that you could use. By drawing your attention to adverts, news items, or stories, your brain is providing you with topical, relevant and interesting speech material. This is undoubtedly easier for you than scouring newspapers the night before the speech to look for something to talk about.

The technique of mental speechwriting is so effective that many speakers' greatest problem lies in deciding what to leave out. In this respect, one piece of advice cannot be over-emphasised . . .

DON'T SAY TOO MUCH

There are limits to public speaking. It is a form of communication not ideal for the rendition of complex mathematical formulae nor for the transmission of voluminous data. A general might use a speech to rouse the troops before a military campaign, but would use a detailed map and a written series of co-ordinates to set out exactly how the attack would be executed. Similarly, if you were calling for a new voting system, a speech would be the most effective way to explain to people why you were convinced it was the right thing to do, but it would probably not be the most effective way of dealing with the precise mechanism of vote transference.

If readers come across something complex and abstruse in a book or a report, they can sleep on it, re-read it and discuss it with friends. They have, potentially, a lifetime to digest what has been written. Even with written material, however, most people find it difficult to digest a mass of new information. When an official report is full of good news for a government, it is usually leaked to the press over several weeks. Governments do this because they recognise that most people will not take in more than a certain amount of new information on any particular topic in one day or one week, and they want the public to absorb as much of the good news as possible. When an official report is full of bad news, however, governments are likely to publish it all at once.[4] (This is often referred to as a 'needle in the haystack' approach.) As Paddy Ashdown, former leader of the British Liberal Democrats, once remarked:

> There is a rule of thumb about Government statements in the House, which is that the longer the statement, the more opaque the policy.[5]

What this illustrates, among other things, is that overloading people with new information in a short period of time leaves them understanding and remembering less, not more. To be memorable, a speech should set out the big picture, justifying its call with the key arguments, the most important facts, and the most powerfully illustrative examples. Don't use a speech to say everything you know about the particular subject. Use it to say, in the best way possible, what matters most.

Just as you should avoid using too much new information, you should also avoid using up too much time. At official ceremonies, business meetings and conferences there may be set time limits. Ask what they are, and stick to them – if you think you might overrun, prevent this by planning to fill less than the allotted time. It is not usually in your best interests as a persuader to talk for as long as you could. Everyone has heard a speech that went on and on, and felt that combination of pity for the speaker and anger at being 'held prisoner'. A speech that goes on too long is almost always more irritating for an audience than a speech that is too short. As Mark Twain once said, few sinners are saved after the first twenty minutes of a sermon.

WRITING IT DOWN
When we speak in this book of putting together a speech, we don't suggest that you should write it out in full before you

deliver it – because doing so would constrain your style and hamper your ability to respond to any new points that are raised. With a few notable exceptions, therefore, speeches are usually much more effective if they are given from brief notes. On pages 111–15 we set out how best to do this.

3. SUMMARY

- **Should I speak?** Think about whether public speaking is the best way to achieve your goals, but don't let fear hold you back.

- **How can I best collect material?** Keep on the look-out for new information, write down your thoughts, and use them later as the material for your speech. Leave yourself time. Don't try to write it all in one night.

- **How do I ensure that the audience remember my points?** Don't say too much. A well-defined, focussed topic is the key to a memorable speech.

- **How should I write down my speech?** Speeches work best when they respond to the mood of the audience and any points which have been raised. It is more effective to work from *brief* notes than from a fully written text.

THE BASICS OF PRESENTATION

DOES PRESENTATION MATTER?
Try the following activities:

- Go to a friend's house, walk to the kitchen, open the fridge and ask, 'Do you have anything to drink?' Then, at a different friend's house, don't enter the kitchen, but ask the same question. Do people react differently, even though the same question is being asked?
- Watch a film made in a language you can't understand. Do you always need to look at the subtitles or do you sometimes understand what's going on anyway?
- Walk into a recruitment agency in a suit. Walk into the same place the next week wearing a T-shirt. Note how people react.
- Ask your friends if their impressions of speakers are affected by presentation. Do you believe them?

The message that a speaker believes he has delivered is not the same as the one that the audience actually receives. Part of the reason for this is that, for the audience, the message is inextricably tied up with their perceptions of the speaker.

The British TV comedy *Yes, Prime Minister* made this point very effectively when the Prime Minister's assistant, wondering what setting to use for a forthcoming party political broadcast, asked the Prime Minister whether the announcement he intended to make was radical or conservative. The PM proposed the conservative version. The assistant's advice was direct:

Assistant: Well, all I can say is that if that is what you're going to say, I suggest a light suit, hi-tech furniture, high energy yellow wallpaper, abstract paintings, in fact *everything* to disguise the absence of anything new in the actual speech.

PM: Then I think I'll go back to my original dynamic
             speech about the grand design.
Assistant: Fine. Then it's the reassuring traditional background,
             dark suit, oak panelling, leather volumes and
             eighteenth-century portraits.[1]

That rather cynical attempt to soothe the audience's disquiet about anything radical and to prevent their 'switching off' should the PM go for the conservative approach was perhaps a little over the top, but it illustrates an important reality. It is not just the speaker's argument which audiences note: they also evaluate the tone of voice, the attitude, the gestures and much more besides. When an audience hears a speech they observe the speaker at least as closely as they follow what is actually said.

Speech delivery is a surprisingly neglected skill. Imagine a concert organiser proposing to hire a pianist she had never heard play. Now imagine, instead, that she had heard the pianist play, had found him to be expressionless and mechanical, but still felt he should be hired because, after all, he *did* hit all the right notes. Or even more absurd: as well as being expressionless and mechanical, the pianist played so quickly that all the gravitas of the piece was lost, and it sounded more like an attempt to break the world record for notes per second than something designed to stir an audience. That would clearly not be good enough. The audience would expect better – and the same would apply if they had come to hear someone speak.

Audiences are, indeed, as influenced by what is too often dismissed as 'presentation' as much as they are by so-called 'content'. They behave, in other words, just like the rest of us: like businesspeople who fly across the world to meet face-to-face with clients they could talk to on the telephone; like juries who decide from a witness's demeanour under cross-examination whether they are trustworthy; like parents who say to their children, and lovers who say to each other, 'Look me in the eyes'. Such an approach should not be dismissed as irrational or unintelligent. Think of the boy who says through gritted teeth: 'I'M NOT ANGRY!' Should we believe the 'content' of his statement, or should we instead focus on the manner in which he has expressed himself? If you chose the latter over the former, don't let it surprise you when audiences do the same.

Having a good written speech is not enough. When a radio advertisement for a loans company ends with the rapid phrase 'yourhomeisatriskifyoudonotkeepuprepayments' the belief is that, though the message *has* been delivered, the listener has *not* taken it in. Far too many speakers achieve the same result by mistake. You need to close the gap between the message you want to send and the message the audience receives. For this, presentation is crucial. It not only affects how much the audience understands and enjoys your speech, but how much they are persuaded by it. The more detailed issues of presentation – such as planning the layout of the room you will speak in, involving the audience and using audio-visual aids – will be dealt with on pages 119 to 142. The most crucial issues in presentation, however, are dealt with here, as they provide the basis for effective speech delivery. These are:

- Confidence
- Respecting the audience
- Knowing the limits

1. CONFIDENCE

Self-confidence is key. Just as few successful boxers have ever gone into the ring thinking 'That guy's bigger than me, so I'll lose', few successful speeches are given by people convinced they will fail. Not only does self-confidence prevent you from being derailed by fears of failure; it also transforms audience perceptions of both you and your message.

We all know the importance of eye contact when we are trying to *avoid* engaging with people, but often forget its importance when speaking to an audience we *should* be trying to engage with. Audiences will find it difficult to follow a speaker who fails to make eye contact with them, and difficult to ignore one who looks straight at them. Likewise, few audiences will persist in trying to hear a whispering speaker, but most will respond well to a speaker who successfully projects their voice. Voice projection, it must be said, is not the same as shouting. The difference between voice projection and shouting is that shouting tells the audience that you are not in control of the situation and perhaps not in control of yourself. Voice projection, which is what actors, opera singers and good teachers use, says the opposite. Eye contact, voice projection, and other outward manifestations of inner self-confidence say that you are not begging to be listened to because you don't have to beg. You have something important to tell people and you know that they will be interested.

If you act as though you expect audience members to chatter and ignore you, they will assume that you behave in this manner because you place a low value on what you have to say. In which case, they will too. Don't be hunched up and apologetic for having the audience's attention. Try to show enjoyment and enthusiasm. Convince yourself of the value of what you are saying and your ability to say it well. The first step to persuading people that you have something worthwhile to say is to persuade yourself.

Three points are worth bearing in mind:

- No one needs to teach you from scratch how to give a speech or argue a point. We all do this every day – with our friends, our colleagues and our families. The 'diamond' is already there. It is just a question of polishing it.
- Though difficult at first, great public speaking is not beyond your grasp. The skills you develop from the games and exercises throughout this book will help to make you a better speaker. (See in particular Appendix 3 on pp. 237–46.) By

the end of this book, you should feel much more confident about speaking in public.

- Last but certainly not least: don't worry too much about worrying too much. A little nervousness keeps you on your toes, and can help spark off creative energy. You do not need to eradicate your fears, merely to overcome them.

2. RESPECTING THE AUDIENCE

Self-confidence and arrogance are not the same. The self-confident speaker believes that he has something worthwhile to say. The arrogant speaker believes that no one else does. Such self-obsession is well illustrated by Kenneth Grahame's classic *The Wind in the Willows*, where Toad plans an evening's entertainment for the neighbourhood:

SPEECH: BY TOAD

(There Will be Other Speeches by Toad During the Evening)

ADDRESS: BY TOAD

SONG: BY TOAD

(*Composed by himself*)

Other Compositions by Toad Will be Sung in the Course
of the Evening by the . . . Composer[2]

Audience members will respond defensively and negatively to a speaker who appears self-regarding or disrespectful. If you want people to agree with your argument, you need first to convince them that you are an agreeable person. If you seem aggressive, arrogant or over-sensitive to criticism, listeners will reject your argument before they have even heard it. Speakers constantly fishing for compliments by asking 'Did you like my speech?' or 'What about the bit where I . . .?' often find people walking away. Many university students have told us of 'switching off' at the moment lecturers demarcate themselves and their colleagues as 'we intellectuals' or 'we academics'. As one student remarked, they might as well refer to their audience as 'you idiots'. Robert

Reich, former US Secretary of Labour, recalls politicians who are no less sensitive to questions of respect. Practising for an important hearing in front of the Senate, with helpers acting the part of Senators, he tried to fight off the hostile questions with well-argued but hostile answers. His chief interrogator, worried for Reich's political future should he attempt a repeat perform-ance at the real hearing, explained what he had done wrong:

> 'Look. This hearing isn't designed to test your *knowledge*. Its purpose is to test your respect for *them*. You have a big handicap. Your whole life you've been trying to show people how smart you are. That's *not* what you should do. If you lecture them, they don't feel you respect them. But if you respond to them with utter humility, they will feel you do. *Practise* saying it. *I . . . don't . . . know, Senator.*'
> 'I don't know, Senator.'
> 'Good! Again!'
> 'I don't know, Senator.'[3]

Audiences are always easier to persuade if they feel respected. Win people over to you, and they are much more likely to be won over to your argument. Your respect for the audience's intelligence and integrity should be apparent throughout your speech. It should start at the beginning.

USE YOUR INTRODUCTION TO SHOW RESPECT

Audiences don't usually hear the content of the first few moments of your speech. They are getting used to the tone and rhythm of your voice, so this is not the best time to launch the crux of your argument. One good way to use the opening moments, therefore, is to greet and thank your audience, and demonstrate your respect for them. US President Bill Clinton's recent speech at the Jerusalem Convention Centre is an example of how this can be done well:

Thank you very much. Let me begin by thanking the Prime Minister for his leadership for peace and his leadership of Israel; Mrs Netanyahu, members of the Israeli Government . . . I want to say a special word for the young man who spoke first – Ben Mayoft – didn't he do a good job?

I'd also like to thank this magnificent choir, the Ankor Choir. I understand we have students here from Jerusalem, Tel Aviv, Haifa, Beersheva, Akko and other cities. Welcome to you all.[4]

Audience members suspicious of US intentions would find it difficult to characterise Clinton as an enemy after that introduction. He went on to call for dramatic changes in Israeli policy, but the tone established by the introduction demonstrated that this was a speech by a friend. Friendly speaker, friendly policy.

3. KNOWING THE LIMITS
As we have set out, presentation can get you a long, long way. It is not, however, enough. Content matters too. If your content is vapid, people will quickly get bored. Politicians who filibuster and try to scupper debates by giving long speeches that just involve reading out of a telephone directory sometimes try to lessen the anger of their colleagues by doing it in style. In general, they have very few friends.

As well as being substantive, speeches also need to be believable. A slick presentation will not fool people whose real-life experience contradicts the speaker's message. When British Prime Minister Harold Macmillan told voters in 1959 'You've never had it so good', it worked because – for most people – *it was true*. In contrast, when Chancellor Norman Lamont told people in the middle of a painful recession in 1990 that he could see the 'green shoots of recovery', they didn't believe him. Likewise, North Korea and South Korea blare rival propaganda at each other across the border, and denounce each other on TV and the internet. Though the presentation of their diatribes is very similar – simplistic, nationalistic and polemical – and though it is easier for the authoritarian North to block out Southern propaganda, many people try to defect to the South, and virtually no one tries to defect from the South to the North. The reason? The South is a rich democracy; the North is a poor dictatorship.

Speeches need good substance as well as good presentation. Speakers would therefore do well to follow the advice of the McCann Erickson advertising agency, which has as its motto 'Truth Well Told'. This is as much about self-interest as it is about ethics. It may be easy to fool people once. It is harder to fool people twice.

Hypocrisy is as dangerous as false promises, if not more so. 'Truth embodied in a living example,' wrote Gandhi, 'is far more potent than a mountain of propaganda based on falsehood.'[5] Your message is not just about what you say. It is also about the images you convey. If you give fiery speeches that denounce the luxuries of the ruling classes, people will be disappointed to see you enjoying them yourself. If you promote your company as an ethical trader, people will lose faith if they read in the papers that your staff have no rights to representation. If you set yourself up high, you have further to fall. Resist promoting images that you can't live up to. Alternatively, *live up to* images you can't resist promoting.

The most recent famous example of people failing to learn this lesson concerned sexual morality. Political parties contain all sorts of people, but they are likely to be perceived by the public as coherent blocks. When US Republicans attacked President Bill Clinton for misleading the public over his affair with a young employee, some right-wingers within the party tried to widen the attack to the actual affair itself. Mainstream Republicans, while claiming that the issue was 'not sex, but perjury', failed to stop the tide of moral condemnation and salacious gossip emanating from people on their side. When several of those mainstream Republicans were shown to have had extra-marital affairs themselves, the public showed little interest in working out whether each politician had been individually hypocritical. The party – *the whole party* – was seen as hypocritical, even though the people making the issue one of sex were not usually the same as those who had been exposed as adulterers. Your message is about more than your mere words. If you fail to stop images of you developing, the revelation that those images are false will be seen as the exposure of hypocrisy.

There is one final problem with relying solely on presentation. If you don't mean what you are saying, then effective presentation is much harder. 'Deliberate rhetoric,' remarks former leader of the British Labour party, Neil Kinnock, 'kills the speaker, not the enemy.'[6] The same goes for deliberate gestures. When people talk of the 'chemistry' between actors, or say that 'there's something attractive about him', what they are talking about are the many and varied subtle cues of body language. Such signals are too complex to be perfectible by mimicry or design. The best route is to believe in your role.

As we said in the Introduction, you don't want people merely to tell you that you are a great public speaker. You want people to *agree* with you. The easiest way to do this – and this is a point about public speaking and not morality – is to say things that you believe to be true.

4. SUMMARY

- **The audience's evaluation of a speech is inextricably tied up with their perceptions of the speaker.** What has too often been dismissed as 'presentation' is at least as important as so-called 'content'.

- **Self-confidence is key.** Don't be hunched up and apologetic for having the audience's attention.

- **Respect your audience.** They'll accept your points more easily if they feel that you respect their intelligence.

- **Know the limits of presentation.** A vapid speech, however well delivered, will still be dull; a dishonest or hypocritical speech, even if you have a great smile, will still get you into trouble. Direct your efforts to both substance *and* style.

BUILDING A SUCCESSFUL SPEECH

THEME
STRUCTURE
CONTENT
LANGUAGE
WRITING IT DOWN

THEME

1. WHAT SHOULD YOU SPEAK ABOUT?

The greatest speeches in history – from Cicero's indictment of Catiline to Bobby Kennedy's tribute to Martin Luther King – all have two features in common:

- The speaker cared about the topic.
- The audience cared about the topic.

Those two principles, empirically proven to be successful over thousands of years, provide a useful basis for deciding what you should speak about.

SPEAK ON TOPICS YOU CARE ABOUT

The most memorable speeches are made when the orator cares deeply about the subject matter. The topic need not be the 'in' issue in the eyes of the world's media, but it must be one that occupies a prime place in your thoughts. As we'll see on page 177, an expert knowledge of your daughter or best friend is the very reason that it's easy to give a good speech at their wedding. Likewise, if you're ever near Park Lane in London, then try visiting Speakers' Corner. Every Sunday this spot is packed with a diverse range of people standing on soap boxes and speaking their hearts out to the passers-by. Some of them are, of course, 'not fully sane', but the vigour and passion with which they speak is a reflection of the fact that they are speaking about matters that occupy their thoughts intensely.

Digressing from your expert topics can cause you great problems, as British Prime Minister Tony Blair discovered when an interview with a local radio station moved on to an obscure parochial issue on which Blair had not been informed:

Interviewer: Now Mr Blair, the big issue down here is the Little Rockingham First initiative. What do you think of it?

Blair: [Pause] I think it's a very good thing.

Interviewer: Really? But the local Labour group are against it.

Blair: [Pause] Well, I guess you've got to be cautious about new projects and initiatives.

Interviewer: But as you know the people are in favour of it.

Blair: Yes, and there are many reasons why one should be cautiously optimistic about these things.

Interviewer: And of course, it's not a bad thing for the *badgers* either – is it, Mr Blair?[1]

Better to focus on what you know and care about.

SPEAK ON TOPICS YOUR AUDIENCE CARE ABOUT

Consumer choice today is greater than ever. Many people now subscribe to 'Daily Me' internet sites which compile news items from different sources on those topics that the user has specified. Many more turn only to certain sections of their printed newspaper. Similarly, the output of broadcast news is changing rapidly, with more consumer items and showbusiness news edging out political coverage – which is unsurprising, given that most people are more affected by the price of their shopping than they are by the appointment of a new Minister for Agriculture. News broadcasters who fail to reflect this lose out to other providers. Such diversification is to be welcomed, as it leaves people free to select the form and style of their news. A consequence of this, however, is that there are fewer and fewer topics that are universally understandable – sex, health, birth and death are about the only topics that are of interest to everyone. (Just take a look at the front page of any lifestyle magazine.) Speech, like television and the press, is not immune from these changes in consumer choice. People are ready to switch off if your speech is unappealing to them. It is best to consider, therefore, *what kind of audience you are addressing* and *what interests that audience*.

Public speaking expert Dale Carnegie once described the secret to choosing a topic that will captivate your audience:

> The entirely new is not interesting; the entirely old has no attractiveness for us. We want to be told something new about the old.[2]

In other words, find the *audience's* favourite topic, and then find something new to say about it. The best-received speeches are like the best-received presents – they are tailored to fit the interests and hobbies of the recipients.

Let us clarify this by looking at a few scenarios. Suppose two different people have been asked to speak about their job. Even with such a restricted topic, let's try to find approaches that may touch common ground with the interests of the audience.

A stockbroker:

To an audience of aspiring business students: 'How to get rich quick'.

To a women's group: 'Women in the City: overcoming the barriers'.

To senior management: 'Our team's performance in the past month'.

A builder:

To an audience of young children: 'How to make your own toys'.

To an audience of homeowners: 'Disasters in do-it-yourself maintenance'.

To a builders' association: 'The most awkward people I've had on my site'.

A famous example of a topic tailored to the audience was US President Ronald Reagan's 'Evil Empire' speech. In 1983, the

Cold War and the arms race were at their height and Reagan had been invited to address a Christian convention. He skilfully used this opportunity to present the Cold War as a war of morality – something far more appealing to the religious audience than a discussion of geo-politics:

> As good Marxist-Leninists, the Soviet leaders have openly and publicly declared that the only morality they recognise is that which will further their cause – which is world revolution . . . Lenin said that they 'repudiate all morality that proceeds from *supernatural ideas*' – that's their name for religion – [and that] 'morality is *entirely* subordinate to the interests of class war.'[3]

Whatever your subject matter, there is usually some means of tuning its relevance to suit the audience. In the majority of cases, the very fact that the speaker has received an invitation to address a meeting usually implies that there is at least some shared interest. In thinking of a topic or theme for your talk, try to make the common interest as great as possible.

2. HOW TO 'TUNE UP' YOUR MESSAGE

In this section, we will briefly consider two powerful devices that can (if circumstances allow) make your speech more forceful, more believable and more exciting. The idea is to make the central theme of your speech that of a battle. In doing so, you can encourage the audience to take your side. The two techniques are:

- The 'Intellectual Outlaw' approach.
- Inoculation.

THE INTELLECTUAL OUTLAW

Intellectual Outlaws challenge their audience to 'think again' about a topic: 'The majority of people blindly accept that x is the case. The truth of the matter, however, is very different.' Intellectual Outlaws use the unpopularity of a cause to make it intellectually enticing. We all like to think we are intelligent (go out into the street with a clipboard and ask people if they think they are 'above average intelligence' and we bet you'll find that more than 50% do). Intellectual Outlaws play on this by portraying their speech as an intellectual fight against mistaken popular opinion. Moreover, in portraying their speech as a battle, Intellectual Outlaws also make their speech seem more interesting to the audience. In short, this technique can help to ensure that the audience listen to, and are persuaded by, your speech.

The 'Intellectual Outlaw' approach is a powerful tool, adored by conspiracy theorists. Thus some UFO-watchers have successfully convinced many otherwise sane people that the military is involved in a cover-up to prevent ordinary people from 'finding out the truth about aliens'. (Curiously, the military never seem capable of preventing the publication of trashy paperbacks that decry the cover-up.) A story which is portrayed as new, radical and something that many people would rather you didn't hear is almost guaranteed to intrigue an audience.

Consider this quote from the British Prime Minister Tony Blair in a speech justifying the negotiations process that would lead to the Good Friday Agreement:

> I reflect on the sheer waste of children taught to hate, when I believe passionately that children should be taught to think.[4]

US President Richard Nixon used a similar approach in 1952. When rebutting allegations of bribe taking, he conceded that he *had* received one gift – a dog:

> . . . a little Cocker Spaniel dog . . . black-and-white spotted, and our little girl Tricia, the six-year-old, named it Checkers. And you know, the kids, like all kids, love the

dog. And I just want to say this now, that regardless of what they say about it, we are going to keep it.[5]

How could opponents of the Northern Ireland negotiations argue that children should be taught to hate? How could Richard Nixon's opponents call for his children's dog to be taken away? Of course they couldn't, and they never did. By posing as 'Intellectual Outlaws', however, Blair and Nixon constructed debates which obliged their audiences to come down on one side – theirs.

The use of the Intellectual Outlaw approach is not limited to political figures. Let us revisit an example that we considered earlier – the stockbroker addressing a forum about sexism in the City. On its own, the evidence she recounts might appear to be a mere statement of the obvious – but *how much more persuasive it is when phrased in terms of a battle*:

You know, recently, a working party on sexual discrimination concluded that, on the whole, women and men were treated as equals by most employers in City financial corporations. On top of that, all job advertisements for the major firms display the honourable rubric: 'this firm is an equal opportunities employer'. Well, despite what these managers and advertisers say, many women's experience is different, and I'd ask you to bear with me while I put over the other side of the story, the unheard story and the story no one wants you to hear.

In other words: 'What I am saying is controversial. If you agree then you are one of an enlightened minority. Let's join forces.'

The speaker has told the audience that her (eminently reasonable) viewpoint is radical and challenges the current dogma. When phrased in terms of a battle between a freethinking individual and a rigid, outdated *status quo*, which side do you think the audience would prefer to be on?

Thus, emphasising the opposition to your viewpoint may help your speech to seem not only more agreeable, but also *more interesting*. The technique is even more powerful when the opposition are as diffuse as possible – in the example above, the speaker referred to 'a working party on sexual discrimination' and 'major firms'. No individual can take offence at such general statements. One can well imagine a director of a major firm sitting in the audience, agreeing with the speaker and thinking: 'Yes, some firms *are* like that, we must make sure ours isn't.' The less specific speakers are about who their opposition are, the easier it is for the audience members to see themselves as allies.

The Intellectual Outlaw technique is also a useful means of adding 'fire' to your speech. Some events do not require the speaker to create their own 'fire' – protest rallies, heated debates and critical board meetings may already be emotionally charged and heated. Other events, however, do not provide such a ready-made atmosphere – a sermon following a hymn or the first speech of the day at a seminar are often delivered in tranquil and quiet surroundings. In such cases, the Intellectual Outlaw technique provides the speaker with a ready-made enemy – a figure to rail against and to speak with passion against. A superb example of this is a speech given by George Canning, a former British Prime Minister, to the House of Commons in 1798. Canning was arguing that Europe needed to be delivered from French domination, and employed an invisible enemy (namely 'those who do not understand what is meant by the phrase "the deliverance of Europe"') whom he spoke against with vigour and passion. As you read the extract from this speech below, imagine it spoken with an impatient tone – like a schoolteacher rebuking a pupil who 'should know better':

The most complete and desirable termination of the contest would be the *deliverance of Europe*. I am told, indeed, that there are persons who affect not to understand this phrase

> . . . I do not envy that man's feelings who can behold the sufferings of Switzerland and who derives from that sight no idea of what is meant by 'the deliverance of Europe'. I do not envy the feelings of that man who can look without emotion at Italy – plundered, insulted, trampled upon, exhausted, covered with ridicule and horror and devastation – who can look at all this and be at a loss to guess what is meant by 'the deliverance of Europe'.[6]

But the important question is whether there is genuine opposition to your ideas or not. As is clear from pages 21–23, we don't advise you to mislead your audience. If, in truth, there is no such opposition then the Intellectual Outlaw technique is not for you. But if your message is unpopular what should you do? The first step is to use your unpopularity. The Intellectual Outlaw thrives on presenting a minority viewpoint: 'Think again about this issue. Become a member of the enlightened few, not the unthinking many' is the charge to the audience. The second step is to admit *straightaway* the issues where you understand and agree with the opposition viewpoint. Open, honest and ungrudging admissions of *certain* facts used by your critics will help to gain the trust and respect of the audience, by making you appear more reasonable and considered. Suppose, for example, that you are a businessperson explaining to concerned shareholders or lobbyists why you do business in a country that has a poor human rights record. Below are four possible speech openings. The first three try to justify the accusations of human rights abuses – and fail. The fourth concedes them but depicts them as irrelevant.

1. 'There are no human rights abuses in Ruritania. Let me explain how the lies were started . . .'
   Hopeless. This makes you sound like a conspiracy theorist or a charlatan. The (sceptical) audience are faced with a choice between your words and those of Amnesty International.

2. 'Our country abuses human rights too, let me give you some examples . . .'
   Hopeless. Audiences are capable of understanding differences of scale. This also sounds too much like a 'two wrongs make a right' argument.

3. 'Human rights is a Western concept. Let me explain a bit about Eastern values . . .'
   Hopeless. This will make little impact on people who have, for example, watched the footage of an unarmed man blocking the way of a tank during the Tiananmen Square massacre. They already know which 'Eastern values' they admire.

4. 'There are human rights abuses in Ruritania. We wish there weren't. We want change too, but we feel – and the evidence backs us up – that this is best achieved by engagement, not by walking away. Let me explain why . . .'
   Effective. This concedes the human rights point straightaway, and demonstrates a convergence of aims between you and your critics. The issue is now one of methods and the debate has moved on to your ground.

The language you use when conceding ground to your opponents is particularly important. Forthright and bold language ('human rights abuses', not 'governmental infringements') demonstrates to your audience that you have fully understood the concerns of your opponents. Don't seek refuge in euphemisms. Thus, Iraqi leader Saddam Hussein's attempts to label his Gulf War prisoners as 'guests' was never likely to convince their relatives and never did.

In summary, the whole aim of the Intellectual Outlaw is to gain a feeling of unity with the audience. It is, therefore, best to admit certain truths up front in order to gain credibility. The audience will warm to your admissions. Once they are suitably disarmed, tell them that those truths, though regrettable, are a separate matter from the issue you will examine in your speech.

The Intellectual Outlaw approach, when used properly, is a stealthy tool for generating interest in, and gaining support for, your speech.

INOCULATION

A series of psychological experiments conducted over the last thirty years have demonstrated that it is sometimes possible to 'inoculate' the audience against future attacks on the arguments that you advance.[7] Good parents use this 'inoculation' every day – they may warn their children that people will accuse them of being 'boring' if they don't smoke, or that strangers may try to lure them away with sweets. In each case, the parents expose the children to mild forms of the arguments that they may hear in real-life situations. The exposure is essentially a variant of the Intellectual Outlaw approach, in that the parent frames the argument as a battle and 'admits' to the points that the opposing side may advance. Inoculation is often best achieved through a role-play scenario. (We will see on page 125 that getting your listeners to participate in role-play or some other activity after your speech is a good way of reinforcing your message.) A model example of 'inoculating' role-play is given below.[8]

Parent: [*pretending to offer cigarette*] You're such a chicken – you're scared of smoking.
Child: [*after guidance from other parent*] I'd be a real chicken if I smoked just to impress you.

Therefore, it is sometimes a good idea to spend some time in your speech dealing with the main arguments that your opponents may raise in opposition to your arguments. Don't spend too much time doing this as you may find that the whole structure of your speech is then shifted on to your opponents' ground. The point simply is this: if there are weaknesses in your speech, it's better that your listeners hear them from you.

Note that the key to inoculation is to use *mild* forms of the opponent's arguments, not a full strength dose. If you present the other side's arguments too well, you may find yourself converting allies to opponents.

3. SUMMARY

- **Choose a good topic for your speech.** The topic should be one that you know and care about. It also needs to meet the interests of the audience. The best-received speeches are like the best-received presents – tailored to fit the interests of the recipients.

- **Use the Intellectual Outlaw technique when speaking for an unpopular cause.** Entice the audience to join an enlightened few, rather than the unthinking many. Admit certain facts up front to gain the trust and respect of the audience, and to appear fair-minded.

- **Keep the audience on side with inoculation.** Try exposing the audience to mild forms of the arguments that your opponents may make. When the opponents use those arguments, they will then seem less novel and less exciting.

STRUCTURE

In the previous chapter, we stressed the importance of having a well-defined and focussed theme to your speech. Now it is time to consider the building blocks of the speech – the beginning, the middle and the end. The importance of structure in speech making is often overlooked, but it is the single most important aspect in achieving clarity. In the more formal kinds of public speaking, such as legal moots or after-dinner toasts, the conventions of the event will set the structure of your speech, because the speaker has a limited and specific job to do. For most types of public speaking, however, there are few formalities to act as guidelines. It is on these occasions that an effective structure is particularly important in making your speech ramble-free, waffle-free and clear.

1. THE MEMORY GAME
This quick game provides an insight into the way people remember and react to new information, illustrating some general aspects of short-term memory. First read the words in Box I at a normal reading pace. Then answer the questions below. Try the same with Box II.

Box I

truth, heal, care, give, Isaac Newton, give, give, give, kind, help, guard

Questions from Box I
1. Cover the box, then write down all the words you can remember.
2. Did you perceive any 'overall picture' from the words?

Box II

He lied to me
He lied to us

He hurt me
He hurt us

He punched me
He punched us

He stole from me
He stole from us

He insulted me
He insulted us

He harassed me
He harassed us

He intimidated me
He intimidated us

Questions from Box II

1. Cover the box, then write down all the words you can remember.

2. Did you perceive any 'overall picture' from the words?

Answers

Few people can recall all the details correctly. Most people will find that they remember repeated words – like 'give' in Box I or 'me/us' in Box II. Most will remember things that were outstanding or that startled them – like 'Isaac Newton' in the middle of Box I. Generally speaking, people recall Box II better than Box I, as the phrases in Box II all hang together on the same theme, i.e. 'he's not a very nice person', whereas the phrases in Box I, although of some similarity, do not form an overall theme. Assuming that your recall was typical, there are four lessons that can be learned.

- Even recalling a list of seven statements is a tough task. *A good speaker will not attempt to overload audiences with material (see page 11).*
- Things are best remembered when there is connectivity or an overarching theme to the points (for example, 'he's not a very nice person' in Box II). *Make sure that the sections of your speech fit within a theme (see page 58–60).*
- The more something is repeated, the more likely it is to be remembered (for example, 'give, give, give' in Box I). *Make sure your speech reiterates the important points, or they'll be forgotten (see page 42).*
- People take note of odd or outstanding phrases (for example, 'Isaac Newton' in Box I). *Audiences remember and discuss the most novel and unexpected parts of your speech (see page 151).*

2. REPEAT, REPEAT, REPEAT

Any teacher will tell you that schoolchildren usually need to hear something more than once before they take it in, and need to hear it again and again before they retain it. Though adults can process much more sophisticated information, we require as much repetition as children do – sometimes more – if we are to *retain* that information. As a speaker, therefore, you will need to repeat any ideas that you wish to reinforce, and any facts that you wish to be remembered. This applies even if audiences are thinking about nothing apart from your speech. However, a large number of other thoughts will also be darting around the minds of your audience. Thoughts such as 'my back itches', 'should I ask for a pay rise?' and 'I wonder if he's single' are strong competition for your speech on the importance of global democracy. Because of this 'interference', you need to ensure that a listener who heard only seventy or eighty per cent of your speech, and was only half listening to that, could still comprehend, remember and *be persuaded by* your core argument. This makes repetition essential.

Repetition needn't make for bad oratory. The Beatitudes in the Sermon on the Mount make repeated use of the phrase 'Blessed are'. American civil rights leader Martin Luther King's greatest speech declares four times that 'now is the time', demands nine times 'let freedom ring', and tells us ten times 'I have a dream'. Black nationalist leader Malcolm X's uncompromising response to King's 'Dream' is equally repetitive, and equally striking:

> This is a real revolution. Revolution is always based on land. Revolution is never based on begging somebody for an integrated cup of coffee. Revolutions are never fought by turning the other cheek. Revolutions are never based on love-your-enemy-and-pray-for-those-who-spitefully-use-you. And Revolutions are never waged singing 'We Shall Overcome'. Revolutions are based on bloodshed.[1]

Dr Goebbels remarked cynically that 'if you say something loud enough and often enough, people will believe it'. Thankfully, this is not quite true, but what *is* true is that if you say something quietly and only once, people are unlikely to remember it. Heard more than once, a message can have more impact. It is for this reason that advertisers spend millions of dollars running adverts again and again; it is for this reason that songs return to the chorus. A point repeated is much more likely to be a point retained.

'TELL 'EM WHAT YOU'RE GOING TO SAY, SAY IT, AND TELL 'EM WHAT YOU SAID'

One highly effective use of repetition is a speech structure based on a preview, explanation and summary of your argument. It works as follows. After making your opening remarks (see page

20), briefly set out what you will be arguing, and why. This helps your listeners to know what they are listening for, and gives them a feeling of familiarity with what is being talked about. The core of the speech will then be much clearer, as your audience will know where you are heading. After explaining your argument, summarise it to remind people what you have said. A powerful summary can provide a highly effective ending, enabling your speech to go out with a bang, not a whimper. The effect is both to reinforce the ideas in the minds of your listeners, and to convey that you are firmly 'on top of' your subject.

American suffragist Susan Anthony's 'Are Women Persons?' speech is a good example of how effective this approach can be:

> Friends and fellow citizens: I stand before you tonight under indictment for the alleged crime of having voted at the last Presidential election, without having a lawful right to vote. It shall be my work this evening to prove to you that in thus voting, I not only committed no crime, but instead simply exercised my citizen's rights, guaranteed to me and all United States citizens by the National Constitution.

She then delivered a brilliant analysis of how, by voting, she had merely exercised constitutional rights that apply to every 'person' – not just 'male persons'. Her conclusion reiterated this message and reinforced it in the minds of her listeners:

> Are women persons? I hardly believe any of our opponents will have the hardihood to say they are not. Being persons, then, women are citizens; and no State has a right to make any law, or to enforce any old law, that shall abridge their privileges or immunities.[2]

Including a preview and a summary can help to make your speech concise, clear and memorable. 'Telling 'em what you're going to say' helps your audience to take in your message. 'Telling 'em what you said' helps your audience to remember it.

3. THE BEGINNING: TELL 'EM WHAT YOU'RE GOING TO SAY

After clearing your throat with a stock phrase such as 'Thank you very much, Madam Chair, ladies and gentlemen', there are two tasks that a speaker should accomplish:

- Make an impact
- Give a preview

MAKE AN IMPACT

First impressions are just as important in public speaking as they are in any other aspect of life. Your opening not only prepares the audience for what to expect, but also *cues how they will respond* to your speech – be it with laughter, applause or awe. In effect, you have to 'win the audience' during your opening, for the image they form of you at the beginning will persist throughout the rest of the speech. Consider the examples below:

Your goal	An appropriate opening
To entertain the audience (*e.g. a best man's speech at a wedding, or an after-dinner speech*)	Start with something short, snappy and funny – perhaps a one-line gag or a statement about the chairman or compère. Visual props also work well – thus, for example, the best man might produce an unflattering and comic photo of the groom. Avoid starting with long anecdotes, as these tend not to create an *immediate* sense of entertainment.

To arouse passionate support for a cause (*e.g. at a public demonstration, or in a debate*)	Start with something dramatic. Perhaps, if demonstrating against some injustice in the world, the speaker might relate a suitable statistic with passion and vigour: e.g. 'Did you know, that as we sit in this big room today, the average animal in a battery farm is confined to a space *less than the size of a piece of A4 paper.*'
To gain approval for your work (*e.g. at a seminar, or when presenting a report of recent work to an employer*)	Start with something confident and interesting. Perhaps summarise the message of your presentation: e.g. 'In my talk today, I will show you that our productivity is up by 20% compared with last month.'

For most speeches, you should aim to make an impact on your audience within the first minute or so. All the suggested openings above aim to grab the audience's attention immediately, and do so in a style that reflects the mood of the whole speech. The audience will be most attentive soon after the start of your talk, so you should hit them with your best gag, or most shocking statistic, or most impressive fact at the start. When a speech begins in a weak and lifeless manner, the audience do not look forward in anticipation to the rest of the speech – they look forward to the end of the speech.

It is a common failing not to realise the importance of a big opening. We have seen plenty of speeches where the speaker begins with a lame apology: 'I was very nervous before this presentation' or 'Those of you who attended the seminar last year will already have heard this'. The reason that people sometimes use openings like these is that they think they convey a sense of modesty, or at least one of informal naturalness. They don't: it merely sounds weak.

Your beginning needs to be high impact, impressive and a reflection of the image you want the audience to have about your speech. Start as you mean to go on.

THE PREVIEW

The opening section is also the ideal time to describe your 'take home message'. Your audience are then prepared for the main section of your speech, and, if they lose concentration (as all audiences do at some point) then they at least have an idea of where you are heading with your talk.

So important is the preview, in fact, that many good public speakers write the outline of their talk on a blackboard or overhead projector, or distribute handouts which outline the main points. This is especially important when the aim is to educate the audience – when delivering lectures or sermons for example, or when teaching schoolchildren about serious issues.

After a preview, the audience should be aware of what to expect from the rest of the speech. Let's clarify what might be in a successful opening. On the left of the table opposite a particular type of speech is listed. On the right is the sort of knowledge about the speech that a listener should possess after only listening to the *preview*.

In each case, the aim is to be able to condense your entire speech into a few sentences. If the topic of your talk is focussed and well defined, then compressing the central message of your talk should be relatively easy. A neat preview of the talk increases the audience's ability to absorb and follow your speech. Think of it as oratory's equivalent of a headline.[3]

Before we leave this section, a note of caution. Some speakers (especially those at seminars and those aiming to instruct or educate their audience) use the start and only the start of their talks to explain concepts and background material that are essential to understanding the talk. For example, the speaker discussing electromagnetic radiation and brain tissue might explain, at the beginning, the technique of ESR spectroscopy

Type of speech	What an audience member may know following the opening of the speech
Presentation bidding to supply computers to a firm	1. BusinessWare is an established supplier of computers to large firms. 2. It can provide a wide range of computers. 3. It can supply computers at low cost.
Sermon	He's going to explain that salvation is by grace and not by works, and how that affects my life.
Speech at an academic seminar	She's going to show the results of her latest experiments on the effect of electromagnetic fields on brain tissue, and what that means for mobile phone users.

that she used to conduct her experiments and then just casually refer to that term later. This is not helpful for the audience. Although an audience might well follow an explanation of a concept at the start of a talk, it does not necessarily follow that they are sufficiently acquainted with that idea in order to understand its application. In other words, it is not advisable to simply 'set the scene' at the outset and then assume the audience will remember that information. Background explanations need to run *throughout* your talk.

4. THE MIDDLE: SAY IT

Following a successful opening, therefore, the 'route' followed during the main part of your speech should be clear and as easy-to-follow as possible. It is always simplest to follow routes that are straight and well signposted.

STEP ONE: DIVIDE YOUR SPEECH INTO A FEW MANAGEABLE SEGMENTS

First, let us consider how you can signpost your speech, in order to make it easy for the audience to follow. Signposting is best done by dividing your topic into a few different segments.

The memory game on page 39 demonstrated that it is only possible to store a handful of facts in your short-term memory, so somewhere between two and five sections is usually ideal. Rather than simply creating, say, three sections for your speech, it is sometimes helpful first to write down all the points you want to make and then see how they could logically be grouped together.

Suppose, for example, you are due to address a gathering of politicians to lobby them for improvements in the treatment of animals. As outlined on page 28, you need to focus your topic in a way that is relevant to the audience. So, in this case, you may decide that your subject should be 'Animal welfare in this country: easy and popular ways to reform the law'. The first step is then to divide the topic into a small number of sections, which may include:

- What can be done to improve things?
- What kind of cruelty do animals suffer?
- What's the current state of the law?

Those sections may include numerous arguments, examples and statistics. The three points, however, provide a clear demarcation of the main parts of the talk, and thus make it easy for the audience to see where you are going. Note also that these sections *support the theme* of the overall talk – there is little point devising a catchy, focussed theme if the sections themselves are diverse and inchoate.

STEP TWO: ORDER THE SECTIONS IN A LOGICAL MANNER
Good signposting is not the only requirement for an easy-to-follow talk. The route that the speaker takes should also be as straight as possible. You therefore need to order the sections so that they follow some logical order. The sections described above might be rearranged thus:

1. What kind of cruelty do animals suffer? (Problem)
2. What's the current state of the law? (Inadequate solution)
3. What can be done to improve things? (Better solution)

Compare the initial order with the better order above – the better order has connectivity between the sections. The speech now flows elegantly from problem to solution. The conclusions are not entangled with the discussion and the overall order is straightforward and logical. Neat, commonsensical ordering of well-defined sections makes it easy for the audience to follow the speech. It is surprising how many speakers never order their points logically – even though it is one of the simplest ways to enhance the clarity of a speech.

The evolution of the structure of the speech looked something like this:

Reason for talk	To lobby for animal rights		
Choose a relevant and focussed topic	Animal welfare in this country: easy and popular ways to reform the law		
Divide the topic into a few sections	• What can be done to improve things?	• What kind of cruelty do animals suffer?	• What's the current state of the law?
Order the sections in a logical manner	1. What kind of cruelty do animals suffer?	2. What's the current state of the law?	3. What can be done to improve things?

A well-structured speech is easy to follow. Dividing your speech into a *small number* of *logically ordered* sections helps to prevent the audience from becoming lost and confused.

VERBAL TAGGING: A LESSON FROM CHURCHILL

Images last longer in the mind than words or numbers. It is therefore often a good idea to provide neat mental images (often called 'verbal tags') that summarise your main points. Perhaps the best-ever example of a verbal tag was Winston Churchill's use of the phrase 'Iron Curtain'. The phrase encapsulates a whole host of images – the curtain as a divider, cutting off East from West, and also the curtain as a concealing device, behind which secret plots are discussed. And why is the curtain made of iron? Because iron is cold and artificial and manufactured by machines, an allegory of the harshness that Churchill ascribed to communist rule. At every level of analysis, Churchill's characterisation gives exactly the image he wanted people to remember. Perhaps, one day, in an age of minimalist home décor, an iron curtain will sound kind of homely, but until then it remains the best characterisation you will ever find.

Many good speakers try to incorporate verbal tagging into their structure. In the example of the animal welfare speech above, it might then be better to 'tag' the fairly mundane subject heading of 'What's the current state of the law?' with something more memorable, like 'The law is full of holes'. Similarly, the heading 'What could be done to improve things' could be replaced with 'Criminal penalties for criminal acts'. Whatever tag you choose, the aim is to provide a neat, memory-jogging way of summarising the sections of your speech.

5. THE END: TELL 'EM WHAT YOU SAID

The advice we offer for structuring the final section of your speech mirrors that offered for structuring the opening section.

An audience will not concentrate fully throughout the whole of your speech. The words 'and finally . . .', however, are a great way of grabbing attention – so the last part of the speech is an ideal place to re-emphasise your message. The summary, like the preview, should be as concise as possible and snappy enough to be memorable.

We examined earlier the importance of using the *first* few moments of your speech wisely. The *last* few moments are even more important, for they largely determine the applause (or lack of it) that you will receive. If you peter out at the end of an otherwise good speech, members of the audience will not find themselves clapping very enthusiastically and will conclude – *post facto* – that this is because they didn't really like your message. If you want to memorise or prepare the lines for any part of the speech, do it for the end.

It is surprising how many speakers fail to end with a bang. Some speakers end with a weak apology for taking too much time, or a series of 'well, I think that's it except . . .' half-endings that make people get up to leave before the speaker has actually stopped speaking. Some speakers, particularly those at seminars, end with a list of acknowledgements. Such a list is unlikely to be the high point of the speech – so why finish on it? Why not just acknowledge the relevant people through-out the talk? Avoid low-impact endings. Summarise your key points and end with something clear, decisive and interesting, such as a pithy remark or a call for action. The last few moments of the speech allow you to cue the applause from the audience. The most vigorous applause comes when the audi-ence wants you to carry on speaking and wishes you had never stopped. This requires you end your speech powerfully – with plenty of volume and passion. A speech shouldn't stop – it should finish.

6. SUMMARY

- **Tell 'em what you're going to say, say it, and tell 'em what you said.** Preview your speech at the start and summarise it at the end. Repetition implants your message in the minds of the audience.

- **Win the audience at the start of the talk.** Greet them in the first few moments, and then grab their attention straightaway.

- **Make the main part of your talk easy to follow.** Divide your talk into a small number of logically ordered sections. Use verbal tagging to make your speech structure memorable.

- **Finish on a high.** Use the end of your talk to cue applause and arouse emotion.

CONTENT

We have established that the *theme* of a speech must be clear, relevant and well-defined. We have also established that the *structure* of a speech should be well signposted, with points separated into sections. We now consider the *material* (such as arguments, examples and anecdotes) that will be built on that outline. There are three main areas to consider:

- How audiences think.
- How to make a strong speech.
- What makes a speech vulnerable?

1. HOW AUDIENCES THINK

Arguably, the only universal principle of public speaking is to *connect* with the audience. Speakers who are connected to, or 'in tune' with their audience will receive the most applause, secure the most respect and win the most minds. When speakers seek to convince, amuse or stir members of an audience, they are asking them to change their behaviour. Changes in behaviour come from within the members of the audience themselves and depend primarily on the thoughts that your listeners generate while you are speaking. Think about a conversation where you agreed really enthusiastically with the person you were talking to. You were probably itching to make your own points as they were speaking. 'Yes, that's right – exactly the same thing happened to me' you might have thought. You were really in agreement not because the other person had transformed your core values, but because your mind was swarming with similar experiences that confirmed the point under discussion.

Connecting with an audience depends on many factors. There are, however, two points to consider in relation to the *content* of a speech:

- How the audience *relate* to your speech.
- How the audience *remember* your speech.

HOW THE AUDIENCE RELATE TO YOUR SPEECH
The secrets of how to relate to an audience have a long history. Consider this statement from the second book of Aristotle's *Rhetoric*:

> People love to hear stated in general terms what they already believe in some particular connection: e.g. if a man happens to have bad neighbours or bad children, he will agree with anyone who tells him, 'Nothing is more annoying than having neighbours', or, 'Nothing is more foolish than to be the parent of children.' The orator has therefore to guess the subjects on which his hearers really hold views already, and what those views are, and then must express, as general truths, these same views on these same subjects.[1]

Relating to an audience does not require that you abandon your beliefs or morals. The Apostle Paul, who helped bring Christianity to Europe, once wrote:

> Though I am free and belong to no man, I make myself a slave to everyone, to win as many as possible. To the Jews I became like a Jew, to win the Jews. To those under the law I became like one under the law . . . so as to win those under the law . . . To the weak I became weak, to win the weak. I have become all things to all men so that by all possible means I might save some.[2]

Aristotle, Paul and many other great figures in history have all realised that the key to great speaking is to focus on the audience. Ask yourself what motivates, interests and captivates them – and there you will find the best way to frame arguments or the best examples to use. As we have seen, Ronald Reagan's 'Evil Empire' speech was successful precisely because it was tailored to suit the audience. It was a speech to a religious audience, so Reagan described the Cold War in terms of a battle for religious morality.

Speakers who remain aloof from the concerns of their audience will be much less likely to win them over. Thus, high office will remain some way away from the aspiring politician who campaigns with the slogan: 'The whole arts world has been let down by this Government – it is time we voted it from office.' The issue at stake is something irrelevant to most voters, somewhere down the list after Sunday trading and relations with Estonia. It might persuade the audience at a ballet reception, but it is unlikely to work magic elsewhere. And it is not just politicians who need to remember this.

In all the examples overleaf, it is apparent that the interests of the recipients of the speech are central. Speakers are most likely to achieve their goals by *framing all arguments in terms of things that matter to the audience*. They need to aim for the 'argumentative baseline'. This is the point at which the audience stops questioning the assertions on which an argument is based. Take, for example, the argument advanced by the person addressing school pupils, that 'If you work hard, you'll be able to buy a fast car when you land a good job in future.' Here, he has reached the argumentative baseline – his audience, in this case, do not question that it is a good thing to have a well-paid job and a fast car. Crucially, however, a different audience (tree protestors, for example) may not have the same argumentative baseline – they may ask, 'What's so good about having a fast car?' In other words, an assessment of the interests and values of the audience allows you to pitch to their argumentative baseline. When the common agreement is greatest between speaker and audience, the persuasion is also greatest.

Type of speech	Goal of speaker	Interests of listeners	Possible arguments or examples
Address to school pupils in the run-up to exams.	To inspire the pupils to study hard.	Perhaps: sport, music, films, dating and freedom from parental/school authority.	Find quotes from sportspeople/ musicians about the importance of hard work. Explain how good qualifications, and, therefore, a good job will give them the freedom they want – perhaps to buy fast cars or exotic holidays.
Human rights campaigner lobbying a large company for support.	To obtain money for human rights work.	At the very least: company image and doing business.	Argue in terms of the caring image of the company that the publicity will bring. Frame proposals in a business-like fashion.
Best man's speech.	Ensure that everyone enjoys the speech and that the bride and groom feel happy and special.	The lives of the bride and groom.	Anecdotes about the bride and groom are ideal. Tease their mannerisms by mimicry. Keep everything in good spirit.

Let us now distill that general advice into some clear guidelines.

1. *Aim for the argumentative baseline* – the point at which the audience no longer question the assertions that lie behind your argument. It is worth noting that during his famous 'I Have a Dream' speech for racial equality, Martin Luther King received far greater applause for lines such as:

> I have a dream this afternoon that one day Negroes will be able to buy a house or rent a house anywhere that their money will carry them and they will be able to get a job

than he did for more poetic lines such as:

> I have a dream this afternoon that the brotherhood of man will become a reality in this day, with this faith[3]

The first quote hit the audience's argumentative baseline – nobody questioned that it was a good thing to have a job. The second quote lay further from it – though if King had been addressing a philosophy convention, the reverse might well have been true.

2. *Talk to your audience in terms they can readily relate to.* That's what British Prime Minister David Lloyd George did during the First World War when he described Germany as

> the road hog of Europe. Small nationalities are thrown into the roadside. Women and children are crushed under the wheels of his cruel car, and Britain is ordered out of the road.[4]

3. *Relate facts to the audience that they already know are true.* That's what Lenin did when he remarked:

> I don't know whether you agree with the Provisional Government. But I know very well that when they make sweet speeches and make many promises they are deceiving you and the whole Russian people. The people need peace. The people need bread and land. And they give you war, hunger, no food. And the land remains with the landowner.

4. *Ask the audience questions to which they already know the answer*. That's what William the Conqueror did when he asked his soldiers,

> Did not your fathers capture the Franks? Did not you in your own time engage the Franks? Did not the Franks prefer flight to battle, and use their spurs?

All four of these devices were used successfully by Sojourner Truth, a former slave, when she spoke at a Women's Rights Convention in Ohio in 1851:

> That man over there say that women need to be helped in carriages and lifted over ditches, and to have the best place everywhere. Nobody ever helps me into carriages, or over mud-puddles, or gives me any best place. And ain't I a woman? Look at me! Look at my arm! I have ploughed and planted, and gathered into barns, and no man could head me! And ain't I a woman?

The most persuasive arguments are not necessarily the most sophisticated or intricate. They are the ones that relate most closely to the values and experience of the audience.

HOW THE AUDIENCE REMEMBER YOUR SPEECH

Most people can usually recall the outline or plot of their favourite films or plays and might also recall some memorable lines ('Remember, the force will be with you, always' or 'To be or not to be, that is the question'). Nobody, however, remembers the entire script. The same principle applies to the way audiences remember speeches. They depart with a general feeling of what the speech was about, and may even remember a few notable lines – but they are unlikely to remember all the arguments or points that the speaker made.

Given that, aim to leave them with the right *overall* impression of the speech. Individual sentences uttered by the speaker are only important because of their relation to the *theme* or *'take home message'*. In other words, the context or relevance of individual arguments needs to be outlined as the speech occurs. We call this the Wood For The Trees principle. It is depressingly common to see speakers who, engulfed in the complexity of the argument they are making, forget to relate their words to the central call and purpose of the speech. It is the *theme* that is important, and you should marshal your arguments so as to support this.

Suppose, for example, that you want to persuade an audience to help save the local hospital that is due to be closed down. You may consider that your strongest arguments are:

- The next nearest hospital is ten miles away.
- The hospital has a specialist ward dedicated to caring for elderly people.
- The council is set to profit from the sale of the hospital site to a nightclub owner.

Given such an (overly) emotionally charged scenario, all the arguments might seem self-evident. But you can enhance the power and memorability of those arguments by linking them to your central theme. Rather than simply explaining that the nearest hospital is ten miles away, explain to the audience that *if the local hospital closes, then emergency medical treatment will be fifteen minutes further away*. Similarly, rather than explaining how good the specialist care for the elderly is, tell the audience that *if the hospital closes, then care for the elderly will be worse in this area*. Finally, instead of outlining that the council is due to profit from the sale of the hospital to the nightclub, rouse the audience with the fact that *if the hospital closes, then quiet evenings will be gone for good*. In each case, the arguments (and the sentences that form them) are best framed so as to focus on the damage to the community threatened by the closure of the hospital. Each separate strand then serves to reinforce the main theme. The audience will remember that there were lots of convincing, separate reasons for why shutting the hospital will harm the community, even if they do not recall what the individual points were. (A clear demonstration, incidentally, of the power of repetition in speech making.)

Throughout your speech, your arguments and sentences need to be focussed on the overall theme or central message, because that is what the audience remember as they depart.

2. HOW TO MAKE A STRONG SPEECH
We have established that all speech material needs to be framed in terms of what the audience will relate to and remember. Now we must consider the *quality* of the subject matter itself and how to make sure it's impressive. Ancient philosophers endlessly classified, divided and arranged rhetorical devices and lines of argument into many different categories. Here, our only concern is what makes a speech 'strong'. The answer, usually, is some combination of the following:

- Insight
- Parallels
- Evidence
- Endorsement
- Comedy

INSIGHT
Consider these two arguments, both of which were used by protesters who opposed the implementation of economic sanctions on Iraq:

1. It is inconsistent to put sanctions on Iraq, but not on Indonesia, which has an equally bad human rights record.
2. When Governments are inconsistent about their use of sanctions, then they appear to have a foreign policy that is based on self-interest. This harms their ability to act as peacemakers or mediators in future conflicts.

The reasoning behind the first argument is that 'inconsistency is wrong', whereas the second shows technical insight and analysis of *why* inconsistency causes harm. It demonstrates a knowledge of the way the world works, whereas the first does not. In short, the second argument is more impressive and carries more intellectual clout.

The best arguments come from informed speakers and demonstrate insight into the subject concerned. In addition, the technical insight needs to be general enough for the audience to see the logic of the argument. A good example of this was given by Richard Holbrooke, the US Chief Negotiator in recent Balkan conflicts, on a BBC Radio 4 discussion programme: 'A point that is often overlooked,' he maintained, 'is that sanctions create Mafias.' What a short, yet brilliant argument! It demonstrates his experience and knowledge of the effects sanctions have, and yet anyone who heard the argument could say to themselves, 'Yeah, I can see how that could happen. That's a good point.' It demonstrates technical insight, yet is not so specific as to distance itself from the audience.

Good examples of perceptive arguments are common in law reports. Take, for example, the following statement by the English judge Lord Scarman about whether courts should look at reports of parliamentary debates if they do not understand the wording of a piece of legislation. Most people might naturally think that judges *should* be able to look at such reports to get a better idea of what Parliament had intended. Lord Scarman, however, argued against this very forcefully:

> . . . such material is an unreliable guide to the meaning of what is enacted . . . The cut and thrust of debate and the pressures of executive responsibility are not always conducive to a clear and unbiased explanation of the meaning of statutory language.[5]

The argument demonstrates knowledge of the link between politics and law, but even people with no experience of Parliamentary proceedings can see what is meant.

It is important to remember, however, that *merely* recounting technical details is no guarantee of intellectual rigour. The details need to be relevant to the audience. In a speech given during World War II, Bishop Bell's case against the saturation bombing of Germany gained little from the rendition of details of Germany's art collection:

> It is said that 74,000 persons have been killed and that three million are already homeless. The policy is obliteration, openly acknowledged. That is not a justifiable act of war. Again, Berlin is one of the greatest centres of art collections in the world. It has a large collection of Oriental and classical sculpture. It has one of the best picture galleries in Europe . . . It has a gallery of modern art better than the Tate.[6]

In a situation of total war, it is difficult enough to persuade people to care for the enemy country's *citizens*. Talking about the damage suffered by their galleries was plain counter-productive. He may have been right on the details, but they lacked consequence with the audience. Not all data is useful data.

PARALLELS

One of the most effective ways of persuading people of an argument is explaining that it parallels a similar issue on which they already have a firm opinion. Parallels – by which we mean analogies, metaphors and other forms of comparison – can often be the turning point of a speech. In courtrooms across the world, lawyers examine the parallels between their case and older cases in order to build an argument on strong legal precedent. Used well, analogies and other parallels can make key ideas readily understandable to the audience. More commonly, however, they are used in such a way as to render the essential ideas unintelligible and woolly. The art is in using them properly.

The worst uses of parallels are when a speaker tries to draw an incoherent speech together with a meaningless link word. For example, imagine a sermon in which the speaker announced, 'So, my central theme is "beauty"' and went on to look at 'the beauty of people', 'the beauty of love' and 'the beauty of experience'. The three types of beauty in that case are not really parallels at all. They represent, instead, a feeble attempt to create a theme from three diverse topics. None of the points reinforce the others and the audience would go home in confusion.

A second common mistake is to draw parallels between incomparable issues:

If we can't trust Clinton to stay with his wife, how can we trust him with inflation?

'Trust' here is being used in two different senses. The parallel is meaningless. Clinton may be untrustworthy as a spouse, but, while that may raise doubts about his honesty, it says little about the effectiveness of his monetary policies. In this case it would probably be more effective to make a parallel between current policies and those in relevant case studies – 'it didn't work then, and it won't work now', for example.

Let us now focus on how parallels can be used to *reinforce* and strengthen arguments. They are best used when *explaining* difficult concepts. The trick to using them is to look for the argumentative baseline of the audience – 'What will they agree with?' Author and preacher Dr Roy Clements, in his excellent book, *A Sting in the Tale*, defines a parable – essentially a type of parallel – as 'a kind of Stealth Bomber, specially designed to evade our psychological defences'.[7] An example of effective use of parallels comes from a student debate concerning the funding of political parties by foreign donors. One side had called for a ban on all foreign donors, and the speaker quoted below refuted this by means of an analogy. The liberal-minded student audience warmly received the comparison. Once this was accepted, the point was too.

> We're saying clean up the whole system of party funding – rather than just banning foreigners. If you think smoking in restaurants is bad, you don't say 'Right, we'll ban foreigners from smoking' – you try to sort out the smoking problem as a whole.

There are two reasons why the analogy was successful:

1. It was clearly comparable to the issue at hand and required no complicated explanation.
2. It appealed to the values of the audience. Banning foreigners (and only foreigners) from a social activity like smoking strikes a heavy note of racism. An audience composed of broad-minded individuals wants no truck with racism – the analogy went straight to their argumentative baseline.

Arguing for restrictions on property rights, George Bernard Shaw used an even simpler parallel:

> A man who holds public property must hold it on the public condition on which, for instance, I carry my walking stick. I am not allowed to do what I like with it. I must not knock you on the head with it.[8]

Such analogies can, however, create a risk when dealing with complex or emotional issues. Imagine a debate on the Middle East peace process that included the following exchange:

Proposition: . . . if my neighbour and I can't decide who owns a patch of land between our houses, we'd go to court and get an independent judge to decide.

Opposition: . . . [*with mocking tone*] and then we had this very profound analogy about the land between two houses. I'll skip over the fact that there probably aren't any settlers on this fictional patch of land, and instead just suggest that international politics in the Middle East is a wee bit more complicated than who owns a hedge.

The analogy may have been drawn with good intentions – not to belittle the problems of the Middle East but to make them seem more accessible. Whatever intention there was, however, the parallel left open a vast area of moral high ground for the opposing speaker to occupy. Much safer in this instance would have been to draw a parallel with a more clearly related issue, like the resolution of conflict in South Africa, or the Camp David Agreement between Israel and Egypt. The analogy used could still work well, however, if adjusted slightly:

> . . . even if it was *only* my neighbour and I who couldn't decide who owned a patch of land between our houses, we'd go to court and get an independent judge to decide. In an international conflict with much greater complexity, fair arbitration is more important, not less. A 'might is right' solution offers no lasting peace.

Thus the speaker could have explained the limits of the comparison, but turned those to his advantage by explaining that these actually strengthened his point further.

Used to support an argument, parallels can help to simplify the complex and to make something controversial seem commonsensical. The ability to *quickly* draw suitable analogies is a hallmark of the very best public speakers.

EVIDENCE

The points we make during any kind of speech – from a business presentation to a street protest – are always more persuasive when supported by evidence. Examples tend to be most persuasive when used to *support* an argument, rather than to *make* an argument. The whole case is most persuasive when there is reasoning *and* proof – like a motive coupled to evidence.

Since evidence is most effective when easily verifiable and easy to understand, examples tend to be more persuasive than statistics. We don't think, correspond or dream in numbers. The graph was invented purely because of our poor ability to manipulate numbers – it is much easier to see a line shooting upwards on a graph than to extract the same information from a table of data. Consequently, statistics are not the most ideal method of shooting your point directly into the minds of the audience. Compare, for example, these two opposing statements – which do you find more persuasive?

1. 'Presidents of the USA have incredibly high moral standards. Only 7% of them have faced impeachment proceedings.'
2. 'Presidents of the USA have very dubious moral standards. Look at Andrew Johnson, or Richard Nixon, or Bill Clinton – all of them faced impeachment proceedings.'

The first statement gives a number – 7%. Most people won't have bothered to work out that three presidents out of forty-three faced impeachment. 'Oh, it's 7%, is it? That's moderately interesting' is the sort of thought it would evoke from a member of the audience. The second, however, is far more persuasive. It sparks far more powerful thoughts from the audience: Bam! 'Yes, I remember weeks of TV and press coverage about them – how could anyone forget Nixon or Clinton's impeachment proceedings?' The second statement taps into a whole box of memories, it triggers all sorts of images in the minds of the audience. The first statement is lame in comparison. Sure, the statistic is more precise, but it would probably be forgotten within minutes.

A similar effect is seen when people talk about time. 'Five years' doesn't seem like very long ago. But 'before I'd met my husband' or 'before I started working at Langham's' or 'before I'd moved to London' do sound like a long time ago. Your husband/workplace/house each triggers a set of memories, which the phrase 'five years' does not.

The first lesson, then, is that statistics can rarely compete with a well-chosen example. One famous exception that supports your point is more powerful than 99 statistics against it.

For some speeches, however, you may need to present some figures. How can you make them seem less numerical and more persuasive? Suppose you want to tell your audience that 84,162 people have signed a petition against a certain policy. Those extra digits at the end just serve to distract the audience's attention. As stated throughout this book, you need to focus on the audience – how do *they* remember information? There is no point expecting them to remember precise numbers – you want to give them an impression of the *scale* of support this petition has. Therefore, '80,000 people' or 'nearly 100,000 people' are both preferable to the overly precise '84,162 people'.

We can go still further. Few people are good at conceiving numbers as large as 80,000. They *are* good, however, at forming mental images.* Therefore, the phrase 'Imagine a football stadium, packed full of people. You look round the whole ground, in every tier and every corner of the ground there are people' is far more evocative than the phrase '80,000 people'. Such pictorial examples serve not only to give an impression of the *absolute* value of the number quoted, but also help to convey *differences* between numbers. For example, the phrases '80,000

---

*A real-life example of this principle is that juries are now invited, before awarding damages, to consider what the sum of money under discussion is actually *worth* – i.e. what it could buy, or how much interest it would bring if invested. The worth of the money is more instructive than the numerical value.

people' and '50,000 people' do not tend to conjure up very different images. The phrases 'a large football stadium, filled to capacity' and 'a small football stadium, filled to capacity' do, however.

It is interesting to note that, although it is hard to visualise the difference between 50,000 people and 80,000 people (a difference of 30,000), it is easy to visualise the difference between five people and thirty-five people (a difference of just thirty). This is because we rarely have to count in very large numbers – we have ten toes, days have twenty-four hours, we live for eighty years and so on. Consequently, we have little visual experience of counting in thousands or millions, so the concept of 50,000 people is little different from the concept of 80,000 people – both are just an unusually large number. You can use this to your advantage when presenting statistics. Suppose, for example, that you are a policeman speaking to a local neighbourhood watch group. You want to warn them about car theft, and will present them with the statistic that forty cars are stolen every hour across the country. You could express this figure as:

40 cars per hour
or 1,000 cars per day
or 350,000 cars per year.

We suggest that the middle statistic is most effective at conveying how high the rate of car theft is. 'Forty' doesn't sound like a large number in this context – we can easily visualise forty cars. '1,000 cars', however, is beyond our usual experience – mentally we perceive it as 'a large number of cars'. Thus, although 350,000 is a larger number than 1,000, it does not carry a much larger 'shock value' – both 1,000 and 350,000 strike a mental image of 'a lot of cars'. However, the middle statistic says 1,000 cars *per day* (a short timescale that we are used to counting in), whereas the last one says that 350,000 cars are stolen *per year* (a much longer timescale that we count in less regularly). In short, the middle statistic packs the greatest punch – it most effectively couples a large number to a manageably small timescale.

The whole aim is to humanise the statistic. A well-presented figure appears more like a story than a maths lecture. Some speakers even like to create a mini-story about the statistic, for example, 'I went and asked the accounts department what the average salary was in the UK . . .', or 'I wanted to know how much this town actually recycles, so I took a look at the Council's figures . . .'. However you choose to do it, the important point is that words, not numbers, are the key to making your point. A word, despite being worth one-thousandth of a picture, is worth a thousand numbers.

ENDORSEMENT

Just as shampoo makers and pizza restaurants seek endorsement from people that their consumers admire, so speakers often use the endorsement of respected figures to win over their audience. In a speech designed to convince (as may be heard at a rally or a conference) supportive quotations can have the effect of calling an expert witness to testify in favour of your case. They can also be used to spark audience interest – as was seen on page 56 when we suggested that a dignitary addressing school pupils might pepper his speech with quotations from sportspeople and musicians. Third-party endorsement can be highly effective. As Aristotle noted, 'even a single witness will suffice if he is a good one'.[9] However, just as a 'good' witness needs to be held in high regard by the Court, endorsement through quotation depends on the regard your audience have for the person quoted. Thus we have just cited Aristotle on the grounds that, being a purchaser of a book on public speaking, you care what the author of *Rhetoric* said. In a book on fashion design, we wouldn't quote him, but we might cite Vivienne Westwood. So too, in a speech to persuade a multinational company to reform its environmental policy, we would quote Anita Roddick (founder of the highly successful and very 'green' *Body Shop*) but not Shakespeare, and would only quote Confucius if there were Confucians on the board of directors.

It is the experience of the authors that often (far too often in the case of speeches at academic seminars) a quotation is used as an alternative to a good argument. Somebody, somewhere, has been telling people that if they quote Baudelaire or John Stuart Mill in their speech, everyone will:

a. Think they are very clever, and
b. agree with them.

However, the reaction of many audiences to such pretension is more usually:

a. 'Oh, so they have an indexed book of quotations', or
b. 'They've quoted Baudelaire out of context', or
c. 'Who is Baudelaire anyway?'

There is a simple test to apply to the use of quotations in a speech. Pretend that the quotation originated from the person you sat next to on a bus and not from a famous philosopher or poet: ask yourself whether, with the quote attached to a humbler name, you would still include it. Often the answer is yes – George Bernard Shaw, Groucho Marx and Oscar Wilde are just three of the many masters of the aphorism. Sometimes, however, the answer is a resounding no. If so, ask yourself how much the name is worth. It is all too easy when writing a speech to fawn on and admire the famous without a sense of perspective. The problem is that audiences won't do the same – unless you quote someone who means something *to them*. Don't quote for quoting's sake. Quote either because the quote itself is noteworthy or because the person who said it has kudos on *that* issue for *that* audience. If neither is true, don't bother.

COMEDY

In the vast majority of cases, a successful speech need not be a funny speech. Jokes are neither necessary nor sufficient. The Gettysburg Address, 'I Have a Dream' and 'We Shall Fight Them on the Beaches' didn't use jokes, and were no less powerful as a result. Jokes can, however, be very useful: they can help you get the audience on your side, as well as illustrate or emphasise your point. As Monty Python comedian John Cleese put it: 'If I can get you to laugh with me, you like me better, which makes you more open to my ideas. And if I can persuade you to laugh at the particular point I make, by laughing at it, you acknowledge its truth.'[10]

There are some occasions, too, where you may well be *expected* to entertain the audience. After-dinner speeches or speeches at weddings are perhaps the best examples, for they are usually expected to at least raise a smile. In addition, Peggy Noonan, speechwriter for US Presidents Reagan and Bush, believes that humour near the start of political speeches is sometimes essential for signalling to the audience that 'This won't be painful, humour is allowed here.'[11] With this in mind, let us now examine what makes humour successful or catastrophic. Humour being a serious business, there is nothing remotely funny in what follows.

First, jokes should be relevant. *Relevant* humour is impressive because it implies that your repertoire is so extensive that, whatever the topic, you can make people laugh. If, however, a joke is irrelevant, there are likely to be less laughs and the humour gained from the joke is less likely to be transferred as sympathy for the core message. Good comics tell stories with jokes seamlessly woven in. Bad comics tell a list of unconnected one-liners. Good speakers will, if they tell jokes, weave them into the speech; bad speakers will tell an irrelevant joke at the beginning to get everyone's attention, and then, believing that the audience has now been won over, proceed with a humourless speech, oblivious to the audience's boredom.

Second, your style needs to be natural. As stated throughout this book, a good speech is a dialogue with the audience, not a lecture. Engage your audience with eye contact and a natural tone of voice. The kind of humour that makes people laugh at dinner parties is ideal. It's quite rare to have dinner with friends and listen to them recite printed jokes. The humour on these occasions instead tends to come from anecdotes ('You'll never believe what Jonah did the other day . . .') or from banter and quips. This is exactly the kind of humour that is best captured in a *relevant part* of the speech. Anecdotes and quips that you *hear* are also far more preferable to those lifted from a book of jokes and stories – for the words used are more suited to a speech. For example, a written joke may use phrases like 'and he replied, petulantly and in a thick accent, "What are you doing in here?" ' – whereas the spoken equivalent would place more emphasis on the tone of voice and use only the words 'so he goes "Whaddyadoin'ere?" ' Moreover, a written joke gives little idea of how funny the joke will actually be to tell. A long, unfunny build-up to a punchline can ruin the atmosphere when telling a joke to an audience, but this will not be apparent when reading the joke in a book. Consequently, the safest tip is to listen for anecdotes and quips that you hear around you (as most people normally do, whether they are speechmakers or not).

Anecdotes are ideal for wedding speeches. Everyone has come to celebrate Kim and Anish's marriage – so they are keen to hear stories about Kim and Anish's lives. The people who usually speak at weddings (bride's father, best man and so on) usually know at least one of the parties well enough to be able to produce some stories from the past. There is a whole lifetime of material – what they were like at school, how they met, what happened on the Stag and Hen nights or even the peculiar mannerisms they have. Think steadily in the weeks before the wedding (or other occasion) and you should come up with many anecdotes. Take care, however, to avoid cliquey in-jokes, the relevance of which are known to only a few. These bore and alienate the members of the audience who are not party to them.

Quips are also useful, providing they are used in moderation. There are one-line quips available for every circumstance – so it is easy to make them relevant to the point in hand. In addition, if a one-line quip in the middle of a speech raises no laughs then so what? It is far less embarrassing than having spent two minutes reciting a printed joke. But perhaps you don't feel like an Oscar Wilde or a Groucho Marx and have no confidence in your own ability to come up with a suitable one-liner. If so, then try the game below.

Inventing One-liners

One-liners generally have a pattern to them. We'll guide you through some of the more common patterns that you can use as a template to build your own quips. Be warned – attempts to 'construct' humour often sound artificial and lame. It is best, therefore, to treat the exercises below as insight rather than prescription.

Extreme comparison

'and I went to meet Garrath at the airport, and then I saw this image coming towards me – with sunglasses and hair like Chewbacca . . .'

'so I threw some cold water on my face and dried it with a towel that had the texture of a Weetabix'[12]

This is simply a comparison of the object under question with an extreme, bizarre but *related* object. Try this one out now. In the space below, write down an extreme comparison that could be used to describe the objects on the left.

Object	Extreme comparison
Image of your partner in their worst clothes	
Worst hotel room you've stayed in	
Most smarmy person you've met in a nightclub	

Theming

'the kind of name that died out in the sixties, like Troy
Tempest or Rory Storm'[13]
'like some kind of strict Victorian father figure'

Theming simply involves characterising a well-known
scenario and producing a strong mental image. Often, it is
best achieved by thinking about the characteristics of one
particular example. For instance, when describing ideal-
istic people, you might say; 'and he probably imagines a
load of children standing on top of a mountain, all singing
together' – which is an image heavily based on an old Coca
Cola advert. The beauty of theming is that you can
continue characterising the object or person in question
until the laughs die out. Some audiences like just enough
characterisation so they can 'get' what you are mimicking
and then laugh loudly to show everyone around them that
they understand the joke. Some audiences prefer the
theming to be drawn out and milked for all it's worth. This
then requires you to be sensitive to how your audience are
responding.

Try describing the most comic or ridiculous aspects of
the following:

Scene	Comic elements
1960s colour schemes	
Eco-warriors	
Freemasons	

Twists

'It was a case of mistaken non-entity'
'Getting money from him was like trying to get blood out of an artery'

The twist is formed by altering a key word in a well-known phrase, thus causing the meaning of the sentence to change dramatically. In the third example, where the word 'stone' was replaced by the word 'artery', the meaning was reversed completely. Try replacing a key word in the phrases below so as to reverse the meaning of the sentence:

Traditional phrase	New phrase
The quality was overwhelming	
They told me about the birds and the bees	

Extreme comparison, theming and twists are just three of the techniques you can use to create one-liners. Don't treat them like a formula, use them to get you going.

Used well, humour can be highly effective in getting audiences on your side and illustrating your arguments. It is important to remember too, however, that you should not feel obliged to be a comic. There are many roads to a good speech: some of them are lined with jokes, some have none; some roads to catastrophe, too, are lined with comedy pavestones all the way.

DON'T PUT ALL YOUR EGGS IN ONE BASKET
The techniques we have looked at can be separated for the purposes of analysis, but work best when used together. Thus, for example, humour will encourage the audience to see you and your case in a good light, but few audiences will be won

over to your side unless your argument is persuasive. Likewise, it is not usually enough that your logic stands up to attack – most people want some 'real-world' evidence too. The most effective speeches run several arguments in parallel: 'cutting welfare isn't just immoral, it's impractical too'; 'the most sophisticated science shows how dangerous it is to ignore pollution, and our everyday experience shows it too'; 'ensuring equality won't just help women – it will benefit the economy'. One highly successful variant of this is the 'even if' argument: 'even if you think it is acceptable to kill a guilty person in cold blood, remember that the death penalty kills innocent people too'; 'even if the company increased its profits by the amount you say – and most independent analysts suggest otherwise – it would still be in debt for the next ten years'. By employing several arguments at once you demonstrate a full understanding of the issues involved, appeal to the different priorities of different people, and ensure that if one argument is unable to convince your audience, others might.

3. WHAT MAKES A SPEECH VULNERABLE?

Just as some lines of argument can make your speech seem more robust, others can leave you open to attack. Four failings are especially common:

- Misinformation
- Contradiction
- Truism and waffle
- Assertion

MISINFORMATION
There is little to be gained from misinformation. Companies that sell dud products don't encourage their customers to return – and speakers who misinform their audience lose credibility. It is not just plain lies that can harm your credibility, but also mere distortions of figures and statistics. In his classic book *How*

to Lie with Statistics, Darrell Huff lists numerous examples of 'massaged' statistics. Worried that his book may appear like a manual for swindlers, Huff defended himself by drawing an analogy with a retired burglar who once published a book on lock-picking: 'The crooks already know these tricks; honest men must learn them in self-defence.'[14] It is in this spirit that we write this section. You may be presented with a false statistic by an opponent in a debate or in a question-and-answer forum. It is thus useful both to know how to handle massaged statistics and how to check that yours are genuine.

The first way of manipulating statistics is by equivocating averages. Often, after a government announces a budget, opposition parties use the phrase: 'This tax will cost the average family ten pounds per week extra . . .' But what is the 'average' family? Let us presume it is one with an income that matches the national average and that has an average number of children. Even then, it is still not clear what the average family is. 'Average' could be interpreted as the mean (the most commonly used form of average), median (which is simply the middle value – so 3 is the median of the numbers 1, 3, 10) or mode (which is the most common value – so if three people earn £5 per hour and one earns £10 per hour, then £5 per hour is the modal wage). The definition of an 'average family' is fuzzy enough for the supporters or opponents of the budget to choose the type of average that suits them best.

However, even if the kind of average is well defined, the statistics can still be misleading. Suppose you are the manager of an airline and you are interviewed on television about the latest accident statistics. 'There is a mean average of one crash per million departures,' the interviewer says. He has been clear about his statistic – he is using a mean average, not a median or mode – but why is his statistic unfair? The answer is that the figure is a smudged average over *all* airlines. If your airline has never had a crash and is diligent about safety, why should you be held to account because other airlines with poor safety checks, leaky engines and pilots with a death wish have pushed the *overall* average up to one crash per million departures? Check your speech for such smudged averages – for it is easy for a questioner to pull one (and therefore your speech) apart.

The second type of statistical fraud you should be wary of concerns in-built bias. Suppose you are a town councillor listening to a speech in favour of pedestrianising the High Street. 'Sixty per cent of people randomly interviewed in the town centre were in favour of pedestrianisation,' the speaker declares. You, as the councillor, should leap on this and tear it apart: 'When did you interview them? It strikes me that if you interviewed them in the middle of the day, you will miss all the opinions of the people at work – the very same people who are probably in favour of keeping the road open to get to work.' The people interviewed thus contributed to an in-built bias in the statistic. It is possible too that the *question* asked of those interviewed could also be a source of in-built bias. A famous example of this was the 'loaded' statement blatantly posed in a Chilean referendum in 1978: 'In the face of international aggression . . . I support President Pinochet in his defence of the dignity of Chile.' When there is prejudice in the question, there is error in the result of the poll.

In-built bias may not even be deliberate. A good example of this is the perennial statement by politicians that 'crime levels are rising'. They usually base this on statistics for the level of *reported* crime. In previous times, when it was less common to insure your possessions, fewer people bothered to report thefts and burglaries – whereas, nowadays, things have changed. A statistic that shows rising crime levels may then be more to do with in-built bias than actual changes in crime levels.

The final method of statistical fraud that we shall consider here concerns pictorial depictions of statistics. We have all seen examples of graphs that are drawn with shortened scales so as to show large dips and rises, or graphs that are drawn with lengthened scales so as to show a constant, straight line.

Distorted graphs (see over for an example) are not the only examples of visually misleading graphics. A more subtle variant is shown in the figure below:

Figure 1: A company is offering to increase your wage from £100 per day to £400 per day. They show you this diagram to entice you. The large money bag has a radius twice that of the small one. This means that the *area* of the large bag is four times that of the small one. However, the bags have sneakily been drawn in 3-D – so the bags *should* be drawn to reflect their *volume*, not their area. If you double the radius of a sphere, its volume becomes eight times as big – so the larger bag is actually eight times bigger than the smaller bag. In other words, the big money bag appears much larger than it actually should do – the company's diagram makes the wage increase look more significant than it really is. (Diagram based on an idea by Darrel Huff.)

We can conclude that it is best to root your speech on reasoned points, rather than statistics. For some speeches (such as business presentations) it is hard to avoid the use of statistics – in which case you need to be thoroughly aware of (and open about) the source and the details of the figures you use.

CONTRADICTION
Contradictions harm the intellectual rigour of a speech. A common technique in public debate is to find contradictions in your opponents' speech and then exploit them. A speech that contains inconsistencies is easily dismissed as 'poorly thought out' or 'a tangled mess'.

Sometimes, contradictions are easy to spot. Take, for example, these two 1967 headlines from the *Times*:

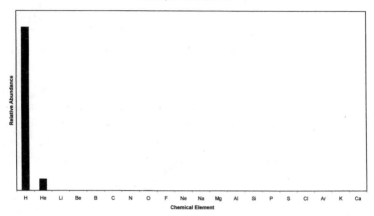

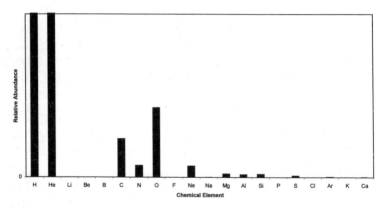

Figure 2: The bar chart shows what the universe is made of. The graph at the top leads the reader to conclude that the universe consists of only Hydrogen (H) and a small amount of Helium (He). The contracted graph at the bottom draws your attention to the large amount of Oxygen (O) and to the irregular nature of the graph. (The scale on the second graph is so short that the vertical line representing Hydrogen (H) shoots off the top of the graph and would carry on for nearly half a kilometre.) Although both graphs contain the same information, the scale chosen for the vertical axis will lead people to very different conclusions.

'NIZAM OF HYDERABAD IS DEAD'

(23 February)

'NIZAM OF HYDERABAD SLIGHTLY BETTER'

(24 February)[15]

It is easy to search through your own speech (or an opponent's speech in a debate) and remove such obvious inconsistencies. It is harder, however, to spot *underlying* contradictions. These arise when the *principles* on which your arguments are based are inconsistent. Consider, for example, this hypothetical speech in favour of voluntary euthanasia:

> It is a fundamental human right to be able to choose when you die. Your body is your own and it's up to you what you do with it. We should allow voluntary euthanasia. Patients who are terminally ill, people in pain and suffering and all people should be allowed control over their own death. All that should be needed is a consultation with two doctors and then a signature of approval.

Let's consider the two parts of that argument. First, the speaker argues that it is a *fundamental right* to choose when you die. Second, the speaker argues that the *approval of two doctors is needed*. The principle of freedom from control that is inherent in the first argument does not square with the need to obtain doctors' consent. The points made in the speech fight each other, rather than reinforcing each other.

Check your speech critically before you deliver it, and attempt to defuse possible sources of contradiction. Let us try to remove the one in the speech quoted above. First, we need to remove talk of 'fundamental rights' to make the issue of free choice seem less rigid. Next, we need to frame the argument for medical consent in terms that relate to the patient's choice. The reworked speech might look something like this:

People must have as much control over their bodies as possible, and that must include a choice of when they die. But we live in the real world. We must also realise that safeguards need to be put into place – for there is no reason why a fleeting moment of mental illness should be allowed to colour the judgement of someone faced with such an important decision. Thus, we would allow the patient free choice, as long as a qualified doctor can confirm that the patient is *able to make a reasoned choice*.

It is always better to soften (or even point out) the apparent contradictions yourself, rather than allow a questioner from the audience or a debating opponent to draw attention to the incongruities.

TRUISM AND WAFFLE

Truisms abound in daily life and are also found in too many speeches. Like the contradiction, the truism has the effect of removing intellectual weight from your speech. It is easy to ridicule a speech that is full of truisms. Consider this extract from the Fry & Laurie sketch 'Dr Tobacco':

Patient: I suppose you're going to tell me that cholesterol isn't bad for you next.

Doctor: What's cholesterol?

Patient: It's . . . well, you know.

Doctor: Yes I know perfectly well what it is, but I don't suppose you'd so much as heard of it until a few years ago. You'd die without the stuff.

Patient: Yes, but too much is bad for you.

Doctor: Well of course too much is bad for you, that's what 'too much' means . . . If you had too much water it would be bad for you, wouldn't it? 'Too much' precisely means that quantity which is excessive, that's what it means. Could you ever say 'too much water is good for you'? I mean if it's too much it's too much. Too much of anything is too much.[16]

It is not *always* wrong to use a truism – particularly if you are trying to demonstrate your empathy with a suspicious audience. For example, consider this extract from a famous speech:

I know war as few other men now living know it. And nothing to me is more revolting. I have long advocated its complete abolition, as its very destructiveness on both friend and foe has rendered it useless as a means of settling international disputes.

At a first glance, the speaker appears to be saying 'war is bad and there should be less of it', which sounds like a truism. However, the speaker was General Douglas MacArthur, the US commander during the Korean War. Dismissing allegations that he was a warmonger, he deftly used the statement above to gain the audience's agreement *before making a more profound point*:

But once war is forced upon us, there is no other alternative than to apply every available means to bring it to a swift end. War's very object is victory, not prolonged indecision.[17]

Truisms occur most regularly when speakers do not have firm points that they want to make. Thus, business presentations and speeches in public debates are usually free of them. However, poetic speakers, or those speaking to inspire an audience, should take care – a speech full of platitudinous truisms is a sure way to bore an audience.*

---

*A rare example of a truism-free speech given at a ceremonial occasion is David Trimble's address on receiving the 1998 Nobel Peace Prize. The speech was so good that we've included it in our selection of great speeches on page 224.

Truisms often go hand in hand with rhetoric or waffle. They are used to pad out insubstantial speeches in the hope of making them seem grand and impressive. But, like many things designed to look grand and impressive (gold bath taps, Miss World extravaganzas . . .) the end result is just tackiness. Take, for example, the phrases below:

'We observe today not a victory of party, but a celebration of freedom – symbolising an end as well as a beginning, signifying renewal as well as change'

'Let the word go forth from this time and place to friend and foe alike'

'We shall pay any price, bear any burden, meet any hardship, support any friend, oppose any foe to ensure the survival and success of liberty'

'United there is little we cannot do . . . divided there is little we can do'

'Let us never negotiate out of fear, but let us never fear to negotiate'

'Ask not what your country can do for you – ask what you can do for your country'

Incredibly, all of those rhetorical flourishes (and others) were crammed into just one speech – the Inaugural Address of President John F. Kennedy. Kennedy could just about get away with using these phrases, as platitudes from a President, especially in those more deferential days, sounded grander than platitudes used by the average citizen. Although Kennedy was praised by the press for the speech, speakers nowadays should note that most people resent obvious cues to applaud.

Abraham Lincoln, in contrast, is an ideal role model. His most famous speech, the Gettysburg Address, was composed of short, concrete statements and not laden with soundbites or hyperbole. Another speech was given at Gettysburg that day – a two-hour, florid peroration by Edward Everett, who was then considered the greatest orator of his day. Lincoln's unassuming speech is still remembered (see page 202); Everett's indulgent rhetoric has long been forgotten.

Politicians, like rock stars, are often intentionally vague – hoping that people will project their own feelings in place of the missing details. Most audiences, however, soon get restless with speakers who pad their speeches with non-committal waffle. An example of the risk of choosing rhetorical bluster over substance was the near universal criticism of President Bill Clinton's second Inaugural Address. Take this snippet and vow never to pad your own speeches with similar meaningless platitudes:

> At the dawn of the twenty-first century, a free people must choose to shape the forces of the information age and the global society to unleash the limitless potential of all our people and form a more perfect Union.[18]

The secret, then, is to be definite and concrete in your statements. A good example of this is the tribute that British MP Tony Benn paid to his colleague, the late John Smith:

> He was a man who always said the same wherever he was. If you heard him in public at a meeting, if you heard him in private, if you heard him in the Cabinet, if you heard him in the House of Commons – he always said the same thing, and for that reason, he was trusted.[19]

Benn could have been more poetic and more flowery. He could have used general phrases like 'honesty' and 'genuineness'. But he didn't – he gave specific, concrete examples. The tribute was moving enough as it stood.

ASSERTION
Every argument (including this one) is based on some assumptions or assertions. Descartes, among others, once wanted to

compile a list of immutable, universal truths that one could refer back to as a solid starting point for building an argument. This is not as easy as you might think, as illustrated in the box opposite.

This is not, of course, to deny that fundamental truths exist. The experiment (*opposite*) does not dictate that when lovers say 'I love you', they cannot be sure, and nor does it imply that followers of religions who regard their texts as infallible are wrong. The point is simply that, when building arguments, assertions or assumptions often come into play. This means that you need to look for what those assertions are in your opponents' arguments. You also need to gauge what assertions the audience will accept.

4. SUMMARY

1. **How audiences think.**
   - *Aim for the argumentative baseline of the audience.* Use terms they can relate to and agree with.
   - *Focus your arguments and sentences on the central point of the speech.* The overall impression is what the audience will remember.

2. **How to make a strong speech.**
   - *Insight*: use your in-depth and technical knowledge in a way that everyone can relate to.
   - *Parallels*: simple, uncomplicated analogies are often an ideal way to *explain* your point, but make sure that the parallels will withstand attack.
   - *Evidence*: use evidence that is easily visualised. Humanise statistics.
   - *Endorsement*: bring in quotations from expert witnesses in support of your case, but don't use them as a substitute for argument. Only quote if the comment itself has weight or the person quoted has kudos with your audience.

A Computer as Big as the Universe[20]

Why can't you devise a list of solid, immutable truths? Such a list would be very useful – if ever you wanted to create an unopposable argument, you'd just look back at the list and create your argument from the statements there.

The reason is that you can't get very far before statements start contradicting each other. If they conflict, the statements are not fundamental, logical 'truths'. Suppose you attempt to write a list of fundamental truths and have started with: 'All hay is brown' and 'Hay is grass'. Now let's add a third statement – 'All grass is green'. That doesn't contradict either the first or the second statement on the list. It does, however, contradict both the first two *taken together*. If someone were going to compile a list of fundamental truths, they would then need to check not only for contradictions between pairs of statements, but also between *groups* of statements. This checking would take a very long time. In fact, if the list got bigger than a handful of statements, it would take an unimaginably long time.

But what if a very powerful computer was used to do the checking? Well, two computer scientists, Larry Stockmeyer and Albert Meyer, once imagined an ultimate computer that was as large as the universe, with tiny processors smaller than atoms, all of which worked at the speed of light. Even such a mind-boggling computer, if left running for billions of years, would only be able to check a list of a few hundred statements!

The upshot of this is that, when we build arguments, we don't usually string together immutable and fundamental truths chosen out of a list, but we usually make assertions or assumptions. And so do our opponents.

- *Comedy*: relevant, natural anecdotes or one-liners that fit the context of the point you are making are ideal sources of humour. But humour is rarely essential.
- *Don't put all your eggs in one basket*: speeches are most effective when combining different types of argument and different types of proof.

3. **What makes a speech vulnerable?**
    - *Misinformation*: this will get you into trouble. Be especially aware of the background of your statistics and possible sources of distortion.
    - *Contradictions*: soften apparent contradictions yourself, before a questioner from the audience picks them out.
    - *Truisms and waffle*: truisms bore audiences. A point is only worth making if someone could disagree with it. Rhetoric and waffle are sure ways to make an audience restless.
    - *Assertions*: all speeches use assertion, the trick is to make statements that are acceptable to the audience.

LANGUAGE

WHY IS YOUR CHOICE OF WORDS IMPORTANT?

- What would be your reaction if, returning from a daydream to listen to a speech, you heard the speaker comment on 'how the intensity of scattered cosmic radiation is so strongly linked to frequency, that high frequency colours prevail at an off-axis human detector'.*
- Why is a finance minister who 'invests' billions more popular than one who 'spends' billions?
- Why does British law not allow the words 'conviction' or 'sentence' to be used in connection with children in court?[1]
- What impression would you draw about the values and outlook of someone who remarked 'it is important in any organisation that a boss knows of *his* secretary that *he* can depend on *her*'?
- What thoughts go through your mind when you hear the word 'impeach'?

Your choice of words greatly affects your chances of getting people to agree with you. 'That's not what I meant' is so common a complaint that it was chosen as the title for a bestselling book on conversation.[2] In public speaking, you may not know whether people have misinterpreted your words unless and until you talk to them *after* the speech. This makes your choice of words even more important. You need, therefore, to be especially careful to choose language that:

- is clear
- supports your argument, and
- sends out the right signals about you

---

*Or 'the sky looks blue' – which, as we will see, is a neater and less pretentious way of saying things.

1. CHOOSE LANGUAGE THAT IS CLEAR

In an ordinary conversation between two or three people, all parties have an equal opportunity to speak, and all have an equal obligation to make themselves understood. If the people you're speaking to don't understand, they can just interrupt. A speech, like a conversation, should be about interaction. What makes it different from conversation, however, is that instead of speaking one-to-one or one-to-two, it is one-to-ten, or a hundred, or a thousand. In this situation, it is impossible for individual members of the audience to have anything approaching the input they would in a normal conversation. Individuals can't 'just interrupt' if they don't understand, so the speaker's initial message needs to be as comprehensible as possible.

When a lawyer is addressing a jury, a teacher is talking to pupils, or a computer analyst is speaking to a group of technophobic business executives, this need for clarity is obvious. In truth, however, clarity is essential for *all* types of speech. Even when speaking to people from your own field, the reason why you are speaking and they are listening is that you have some information or an analysis, which they do not have. If nothing in your speech required explanation, there would be little need to give the speech at all.

One of the commonest reasons that people are unclear is that they over-dramatise their speech and use the sort of overly florid and outdated styles of speaking that were prevalent among 'Great Orators of Yore'. Language nowadays is much more down-to-earth. A century and a half ago, Sir George Robinson assured British Prime Minister Lord Palmerston: 'I trust it is not necessary for me to add anything like an assurance of the most profound deference and respect with which I shall implicitly obey and execute the very spirit of such instructions as I may have the honour to receive.'[3] Nowadays, you would just say: 'You can count on me.' Even people who learnt English at Beijing University in the 1970s (first phrase, 'control of the means of production'; second phrase, 'how do you do?') are much more likely to tell you that they 'liked your speech' than that their 'atypical elation was predominantly a combined function of your analytical framework and rhetorical dexterity'.*

There is little, either, that can be gained from jargon. Using jargon is like talking in a foreign language – a language of a professional group or academic discipline rather than a country, but still alien to those who don't use it. Lecturers who can't get their point across in a clear way are not 'eccentric geniuses'. They're just socially dysfunctional. However endearing they may be, they are rarely *influential*. (Note that they never blame themselves for this: it is always, they say, the fault of the public for 'not having the patience to listen'. Note too, however, that a public without the patience to listen to the original argument is unlikely to have the patience to listen to the complaint.)

Speakers who insist on using long words where short ones will do, and jargon or verbosity where vernacular will do, find themselves unable to communicate effectively. There is a story about a prosecution lawyer who was totally unable to get through to the defendant. 'Do you consider yourself to be a "good egg", young man?' he asked. The defendant, not used to such arcane language, made clear he didn't understand what the lawyer was saying. The lawyer tried again, 'A GOOD EGG – do you consider yourself to be one?' But a slower explanation did not aid the defendant's understanding, so the lawyer tried again: 'What I mean is – do you consider yourself to be a member of the *jeunesse dorée*?' A message uncommunicated may as well have been left unsaid.

Imagine you are a politician at a town hall meeting, explaining why you support a liberal line on issues of sex or drugs. Here are three ways of saying roughly the same thing:

---

*Small words have an added bonus in that they're actually easier to say. It is surprisingly common to hear a speaker 'trip' over certain words – like 'legislature' or 'reciprocity'. Such words pose no threat until you try to read them from your notes.

- In a secular polis, jurisprudence should be consequentialist, not deontological.
- In a society without an official creed, the illegality of any action should be determined by consequence, not by religious disapproval.
- In a country with no state religion, actions shouldn't be made illegal just because individual religious groups think that they are sins. Actions should only be illegal if they hurt people.

None of the above is more intellectually sophisticated than the others. The first one takes the least time to say. The last one is the easiest to understand. Remember that the point of a speech is not usually to persuade people that you are clever but to persuade them to *agree* with you. An audience that does not understand you cannot really agree with you. In addition, a good sign that people know their subject well is their ability to explain it to people who don't. At best, speakers confined to specialist language will alienate their audiences; at worst, they will lose credibility. For speakers unable to break their love affair with insider's jargon, one compromise option is this: first, make your point in 'high' English, then make your point in clear English. For the example above, the result would sound something like this:

> [*High English*:] One key principle of modern lawmaking is that, in a secular polis, jurisprudence should be consequentialist, not deontological. [*Then clear English*:] What that means, roughly, is that, in a country with no state religion, actions shouldn't be made illegal just because individual religious groups think that they are *sins*. Actions should only be made illegal if they *hurt* people.

As is clear from this example, clear speaking is not an alternative to intelligent discourse; it is, instead, an *enabler* of intelligent discourse. If you want your audience to understand your argument clearly, you must express it clearly in your speech.

But won't removing complex and sophisticated language diminish the rhetorical power of the speech? No, it won't. As President Reagan's speechwriter Peggy Noonan remarks, big events are often expressed by small words: 'I love you'; 'It's a boy'; 'He's dead.'[4] Simplicity, not pretension, conveys true gravitas. Abraham Lincoln's magnificent Gettysburg Address, it has been noted, contains '271 words, of which 251 have only one or two syllables'.[5] George Bernard Shaw, in a speech on his seventieth birthday, also noted the power of simple language:

> After Shakespeare's death . . . all the middle classes generally wrote magnificent songs about the greatness of Shakespeare. Curiously enough, the only tribute ever quoted or remembered today is the tribute of the bricklayer who said: 'I liked the man as well as anybody did this side of idolatry.'[6]

There is no trade-off between clarity and greatness. Small words do not prevent great oratory. In fact, they can be the *making* of great oratory. In contrast, an audience confused is an audience unmoved.

2. CHOOSE LANGUAGE THAT SUPPORTS YOUR ARGUMENT

As well as being clear, the language you use should support your argument. Words are *not* neutral, they are value-laden. It is best therefore, to pick the ones that reinforce your argument. For many people, that sounds like pointless fiddling. Words are just words, aren't they? 'A rose by any other name would smell as sweet.' Well, maybe not. Consider the following arguments about sovereignty:

> The Falklands have always been British.
> The British occupation of the Malvinas is illegal.

Londonderry should stay British.
Derry should be freed from the British.

Some words are obviously value-laden: 'illegal occupation' is bad, 'freeing' is good. 'Always British' and 'stay British', on the other hand, suggest a 'natural' state of affairs. But what of the places being discussed? 'The Falklands' is the British name: by making that *the* name you reinforce the legitimacy of those who named them so. If you call them 'The Malvinas' or – one step further – '*Las* Malvinas', you reinforce the sense that these are Latin American islands, and that Britain has no rights to them. In the second example, that of Londonderry versus Derry, the first name actually contains the word 'London': doesn't such a place sound very British?

India wants a permanent seat on the UN Security Council. It claims that this would be in the interests of the whole Indian sub-continent. Pakistan disagrees. Furthermore, it argues, there is no 'Indian sub-continent'. There is only 'South Asia', in which the main players are India *and* Pakistan.

Israel belongs to the Israelis. Palestine belongs to the Palestinians. The territory is the same. Some believe Jerusalem belongs to the Sons of Abraham. Others believe that Jerusalem belongs to the Sons of Ibrahim. Abraham and Ibrahim were the same person. So why fight? Because words matter.

Words matter because, in making a choice of words, we are also making a choice of *concepts*. The International Labour Organisation recently published a document saying that *child labour* was bad but *child work* could be good. When translated into Bengali the document was absurd. Child labour and child work were translated into the same Bengali word, and that single word was, therefore, described as both good *and* bad. The message was passed on to the ILO. 'Find new words,' the ILO responded, 'one word for jobs like doing a newspaper round or helping to milk the cows; and another word for jobs that are hazardous, damaging to health, or overly burdensome.' In other words, one word for work that helps children to develop, and another word for work which merely exploits them.[7] Different concepts – different words.

DIFFERENT CONCEPTS – DIFFERENT WORDS

Everyone can be aware of the resonances that words have, but many never give it enough thought. Most people find that, as they become more experienced and natural at public speaking, they also become more aware of the precise form of words they use. It is therefore quite useful to see some examples of how words can be used either to reinforce or to weaken an argument. In the table below are a list of words and phrases. Those on the left appear to be 'bad', those on the right appear to be 'good'. Though both the words on the left and the words on the right can be used to describe the same policies, the image that they create is vastly different.

'Bad'	'Good'
Pandering to populism	Doing what the vast majority want
Doing what the elite want	Doing what the experts advise
Simplistic: the easy option	Simple: easy to accomplish
Low labour protection standards	Flexible labour regulations
Red tape	High labour protection standards
Party political control	Democratic accountability
Unaccountable	Independent

Words do much more, of course, than suggest whether something is good or bad. They also suggest, for example, whether something is important or unimportant. Very few people care about 'the electoral system', but most are concerned about 'the way we choose our government'. Only an economist cares whether pensions are 'index-linked', but everyone wants pensions that are 'inflation-proof'. A previously unexceptional issue becomes big news in the United States once it acquires the suffix '-gate': thus came Zippergate, Whitewatergate, Filegate, and Irangate. Effective communicators use words that demonstrate not only that their proposals are positive but also that their proposals are important.

MISTAKES DO MATTER

Choosing the wrong words can seriously damage your argument. In November 1998, US Attorneys-General announced a settlement between a number of states and tobacco companies that secured over 200 billion dollars to spend on health care and health promotion. Impressive. But how was the settlement described? Badly. 'This is a great day for Attorneys-General.' A great day for Attorneys-General! How many American anti-smokers are likely to be brought to the height of rapture by being informed that it is a great day for Attorneys-General?

It is possible that the spokesperson was aiming her remarks only at the Attorneys-General of other states, whom she wanted to join the deal. But it is more likely that she had spent so long in the nitty-gritty of the argument that she temporarily forgot the wider political and public-interest backdrop to the issue. Try replacing the last word in the sentence: 'This is great day for *cancer sufferers/health care/tax payers/children/America/the victims of the tobacco barons.*' All of the suggested words have their own rhetorical disadvantages – the constant invocation of 'for children' and 'for America', for example, has turned such battle cries into clichés. All of them, however, appear to work better than the painfully limp 'great day for Attorneys-General', and all of them would have secured stronger popular support. A rose by any other name might not sell so well.

One way to check that your language reinforces your argument is to ask yourself what is the most negative interpretation that could be made of your words – the same rule of caution we all apply when meeting prospective parents-in-law or important clients. Alternatively, ask your friends what impression they draw from a particular choice of words, and revise your speech in line with their advice. Make sure they are critical – even overly critical. The end result will be a much better chance of your speech being effective.

THE COMPANY THAT YOUR WORDS KEEP

Another good way to see the resonances that may be carried in your words is what some lawyers and Latin obsessives would call the *noscitur a sociis* test, or 'know a word by the company it keeps'. Thus many companies try to prevent certain shops from storing their goods because they know that the images of the *neighbouring* products can have an effect on their product. If people see an 'exclusive' aftershave in the stores of a budget chain, they may cease to regard it as so exclusive – even if the product and price are identical. Similarly, many of us have experienced that feeling, when reading a newspaper, of 'seeing' a word that isn't actually there, as we have instead read in a word from the line before or the line afterwards. On one occasion, when British papers were prevented from publishing details of a sex scandal affecting a prominent MP, one newspaper made use of this effect by printing a big picture of the MP in relation to a completely different story, but right next to an article headlined 'Scandal Brewing at Westminster'. Surrounding words and phrases can often 'interfere' with a meaning.

The same is true of spoken words – many people appreciate the meaning of individual words, but fail to see that the surrounding material also has an effect on the message. On a recent discussion programme on American TV, a guest complained that the American political system was 'too dominated by powerful lobbies: the gun lobby, the tobacco lobby, the Israeli lobby'. A viewer rang up to complain that it was offensive to compare supporters of Israel with gun and tobacco companies. The guest speaker replied that he wasn't saying that the lobbies were morally equivalent, just that he didn't like the whole system. He went on: 'All I'm saying is that the gun lobby and the green lobby and the others have too much power for people who haven't been elected.' Right on cue, the next caller attacked him for being 'against the environment'. His point about lobbies was completely lost – instead he alienated people by carelessly placing a series of different images right next to each other. The company that your words keep is important.*

HOW THE BEST SPEAKERS DO IT

A good example of effective language use can be seen in the televised address given by Australian Prime Minister John Howard in September 1999, as Australia dispatched 2,000 peacekeeping troops to East Timor. It was, remarked Howard, 'our nation's largest military involvement for more than thirty years'.[8] This is, of course, a factual statement. But it is more than a factual statement. It is a statement that conveys the infrequency with which the Australian military is deployed. What the listeners heard was: *We do this very rarely. The fact that we are doing it is an indicator of how important this operation is.* A less skilled communicator might have put the same thing somewhat differently. 'The sending of troops to East Timor is our nation's largest military involvement since Vietnam.' What the listeners would have heard in that case was: *The last time we tried something like this it was a catastrophe. No one has tried it since for over thirty years. I am the first.* Howard chose his words with care. His language reinforced his argument by focussing on how rarely Australia became militarily involved and not on what happened last time.

---

*A similar principle applies when writing speeches for others. Speechwriters need to choose words which fit with the persona and character of the person delivering the speech.

One of the most effective ways in which language can be used to reinforce your argument is through the use of images. Almost all religions use parables because they help to make the divine comprehensible. Politics, business and technology can sometimes seem almost as confusing as divinity. Images bring them down to earth. Mohammed spoke of a 'narrow bridge over the abyss of hell'. Businesswomen criticise the 'glass ceiling' that holds women back from top jobs. Information technology, it is said, will bring about a 'global village'. As well as being expressive, such images are also easy to remember.

Word play, too, is very useful. Songs, poems, proverbs and rap are all full of word play. Political and social activists use word play to build slogans. Effective slogans should be easy to grasp, easy to remember, and sound like common sense, as in: 'Coughs and sneezes spread diseases', 'Careless talk costs lives' and 'Outcomes matter more than incomes'. What France needed in 1789 were 'Liberté, Egalité, Fraternité'. What Britain needed in 1918 were 'Homes fit for heroes'.[9] In 1318, during the Peasants' Revolt in England, radicals questioned the class divisions of lords, gentlemen and peasants by asking: 'When Adam delved and Eve span, who was then the gentleman?'

Your language should reinforce your argument not only conceptually but also by making it easy to grasp and easy to remember. In addition, as we shall now see, it should send out the right signals about *you*.

3. CHOOSE LANGUAGE THAT SENDS OUT THE RIGHT SIGNALS ABOUT YOU

The words we use send out signals about the way we view the world. Consider the following typical conversation between two people on a bus:

A: 'I have to go and pick up my child.'
B: 'Oh. How old is it?'

'It'! Imagine referring to an *adult* as 'it'. 'I have to go to see my doctor.' 'Oh. Where is its office?' It is not because we don't know the gender of the absent child that we call him or her 'it'. We don't know the gender of the absent doctor either, but we would never refer to a doctor as 'it'. We call children – and never adults – 'it' because, subconsciously, we often *see* them as a gender-less 'it's. Is that how kids see themselves? Absolutely not. For children, gender is certainly relevant. They would never refer to a classmate as 'it'.[10] Indeed, even the difference between being 6 and being 6 ½ is important – a point that adults often fail to grasp. Our language, in other words, shows that we bracket all children together in ways they never bracket themselves. It reveals our assumptions. And it really winds up children. If we want to improve our relations with children, we might consider the way we talk about and to them.

Earlier, we gave examples of different ways of referring to the same places: Falklands/Malvinas, Derry/Londonderry, Indian sub-continent/South Asia and Israel/Palestine. When speaking to people who have yet to make up their minds, your choice of these words can reinforce your argument. When speaking to people who have *already* made up their minds, your choice of words will be interpreted primarily as a sign of which *side* you are on. If you tell a Pakistani trade or governmental delegation that you are keen to invest in the 'Indian sub-continent', you will not win friends. You will seem at best Indo-centric, at worst anti-Pakistani. Likewise, it is much safer to talk of 'Peace in the Middle East' than peace in 'Israel' or 'Palestine'. When US President Bill Clinton visited Derry/Londonderry in 1995, he faced a big dilemma. What should he call it? 'Hello. It's wonderful to be here in Derry'? People who backed continued British rule in Northern Ireland would have seen him as an enemy. 'Londonderry'? People who *opposed* British rule in Northern Ireland would have condemned him for selling them out. Then an aide pointed something out. The official name of the *city* was Londonderry, but the official name of the *county* was Derry. All he had to do to look even-handed was declare how pleased he was to be in the city of Londonderry, county Derry. In the end he got it the wrong way round, but it didn't matter. People understood that he was trying to be fair, and his reception from all sides was very warm.

It does not matter whether the language you use is intended as offensive; it only matters whether it is perceived as offensive. Very few people, for example, like being referred to as non-'x': 'non-European', 'non-Christian', 'non-mainstream'. Nonetheless, some stubborn folk refuse to reform their language. It's all so 'politically correct', they complain, and persist in using language that offends, as a deliberate point of principle. Such people are setting themselves up as martyrs, and as everyone knows, martyrs may either be wrong or right, but they are not known for an impressive rate of survival. You follow them at the risk of your own credibility.

Exactly the same issues apply to sexist language. Where possible, avoid it. There is a problem with English when it comes to 'he' and 'she', because you have to choose one or the other. Sometimes you can get around the issue through pluralisation. Other times, however, you have to make a choice, and there are no easy answers. Some people fill their speeches and writings with the well-meaning but ugly 'he/she'. Others argue, as the old joke goes, that 'he' embraces 'she'. Still others distribute 'he' and 'she' at random, and the fringe invent words like 'se' as a new genderless pronoun. Our sense is that 'they' is becoming more and more acceptable as a singular form for a man or a woman. Thus a police chief might advise officers, 'A police officer's relationship with "their" colleagues is a key determinant of how well "they" perform.' There is, as yet, no consensus on this usage. It depends on you. What must be stressed, however, is that people will make judgements about you partly on this basis.

Is this just about gender and ethnicity? No, it isn't. In all sorts of situations, language that a speaker assumes to be neutral or even positive will be heard by listeners as offensive or demeaning. A speaker who begins a speech with the word 'welcome' may think that is a nice way to begin. It is, in a way. But if you are the guest and the audience are your hosts, it could be seen as presumptuous. 'How can she welcome us to our *own* club/conference/church? The cheek!' Language choice is important for every speaker, every audience and every speech.

In 1992, US President George Bush attempted to regain support from his rival Bill Clinton by launching a campaign around the slogan 'Who do you trust?' The Good Grammar Brigade immediately launched an assault on Bush in the broadsheet press. Their argument was rooted solely in Latin grammar: 'Who' is the nominative form. 'Whom' is the accusative form. For this reason, they argued, the question should not be 'Who do you trust?' but '*Whom* do you trust?' Yale-educated Bush was unimpressed. He knew his Latin grammar. He understood the argument for using 'whom'. More important, however, was the *politics*: only upper-class people say 'whom'. Using 'whom' would have made Bush look elitist and detached from the way most people talk and think.[11] The social and political resonances of the words he used mattered more than their grammatical 'accuracy'.*

What matters most in politics, argued British historian Sir Lewis Namier, are the underlying emotions, 'the music, to which ideas are a mere libretto, often of very inferior quality'.[12] Namier, though often accused of cynicism, was right – the language we use can seem to convey more about us than the actual arguments we make. This is because arguments are things that are sweated over, crafted and prepared, but language choice is assumed to reveal the 'real you'. Former US Secretary of

---

*An old British joke about a phone conversation makes the same point:

A: 'To whom do you wish to speak?'

B: 'It's OK, I've got the wrong number.'

A: 'How do you know?'

B: 'Because I don't know anyone who says "whom".'

Labour Robert Reich had an interesting way of separating 'good' companies from 'bad' ones. He called it his 'Pronoun Test':

> I ask front-line workers to tell me about the company, and I listen for the pronouns. If the answers I get back describe the company as 'they' and 'them', I know it's one kind of place; if the answers feature 'we' and 'us', I know I'm in a new world.
>
> It doesn't much matter what's said. Even a statement like 'They aim for high quality here' gives the game away. The company still flunks. Workers don't feel a personal stake. Employees still regard the company as *they* – perhaps benevolent, perhaps evil, but unambiguously on the other side of a psychological divide.[13]

If our choice of language really is involuntary, as Reich implies, what's the point of discussing all this? Because it is *not* involuntary. It is just *perceived* to be involuntary. Once speakers understand how language is understood, they can change their language. Thus, political consultant Mike Murphy advised US Republicans, 'We have to stop wrapping our cookies in barbed wire.'[14] Your choice of words can be a bit like your choice of wrapping. Cookies are usually much more popular if they are wrapped up to look like cookies.*

4. SCENARIOS

To indicate how some of this theory can be put to practical use, we will end this chapter by examining three hypothetical situations and see how your choice of language can be geared

---

*Interestingly, Mike Murphy's advice is itself an example of effective language. As well as using a clear and memorable image – cookies in barbed wire – he also invokes the pronoun 'we'. Subtext: he is not advising Republicans as an outsider, but as one of them. (We don't, of course, advise wrapping up barbed wire as cookies. Once people take a bite, they will find out, and it will be difficult to regain their trust. See our comments on the limits of presentation on page 21.)

towards winning over your audience. The example scenarios only scratch the surface of this complex field, but they should, at least, provide a few pointers.

SITUATION I: CHAIRING NEGOTIATIONS

You are chairing some tough negotiations between two bitterly feuding parties – they might be companies, they might be political groups. The two sides are being obstinate and the people most affected by the feuding, but not present at the negotiations, want to hear that the feud is over. On pages 159–76 we will examine the conduct of negotiations a bit more closely. For now, we are interested in the language you should use as a chair or convenor of negotiations – specifically, whether you talk of 'bargaining' or 'compromise'.

We suggest that you describe the negotiations in different ways to different people. When trying to get the obstinate parties to budge, you want to tell them what *they* will get out of the negotiations. 'Bargaining' is then the right word for the job – it tells them what they get in return for giving a little ground. When talking to the people outside, however, you want to tell them that there is a peaceful calm between the parties, rather than a squabble for the best deal they can get. 'Compromise' is then the right word for the job – it accentuates the fact that the parties have reached consensus, and doesn't imply that they've got anything more in return than a simple end to the feuding. Each party can piously claim that 'we compromised for the sake of peace'.

In a lovely satire on the British preference for 'compromise' over 'bargain', Hungarian-born George Mikes remarked:

> Wise compromise is one of the basic principles and virtues of the British. If a continental greengrocer asks fourteen drachma for a bunch of radishes, and his customer offers two, and finally they strike a bargain agreeing on six, this is just the low continental habit of bargaining; on the other

hand, if British workers claim a rise of four shillings per day, and the employers at first refuse even a penny, but after six weeks' strike they agree to a rise of two shillings per day – that is yet another proof of the British genius for compromise. Bargaining is a repulsive habit, compromise is one of the highest human virtues.[15]

The processes involved in 'bargaining' and 'compromising' are essentially the same. The primary difference between the two words is the signals they send out about *you*. No one likes 'bargainers', everyone likes 'compromisers'.

SITUATION II: MAKING A POLICY PROPOSAL

You are speaking to a community group about a policy concerning fifteen- to twenty-year-olds. Whether your policy is liberal or authoritarian, the key language issue is the same: How should you refer to the people for whom your policy is designed?

If you remark that 'we have failed to address the problems faced by our young people', you appear to your audience to be proposing something much more sympathetic than if you declare that 'something must be done about these youths', *even if you go on to advocate the same policy* – be it more community football pitches or the re-institution of National Service. A 'youth' may be the same in a literal sense as a 'young person', but the perception is that 'youths' mug people (perhaps because they have problems), whereas 'young people' – especially 'our young people' – have problems (which perhaps make them mug people). Former British Home Secretary Jack Straw talked about 'stopping lads from getting themselves into trouble' – a consciously nuanced choice of words that allowed liberals to see that he cared and authoritarians to see that he was tough. Language choice was central to his project to establish a consensus on these issues. It is key, too, to the effectiveness of any speech you give – be it a policy speech to the community or a presentation at work.

SITUATION III: EXPLAINING YOUR SIDE OF THE STORY

You are a spokesperson for the UK Government, giving a press conference to explain why a European Union deal has fallen apart. The Government's position is that the deal was wrecked by the French. How do you best express that position?

It is tempting, especially when angry, to say something like

The agreement was destroyed by French duplicity.

This may be risky, however. A phrase like 'French duplicity' means more to listeners than the grammarians will admit. It means that you don't like French people. In the speech about East Timor to which we referred earlier, Australian Prime Minister John Howard remarked, 'Australia's quarrel is not with the Indonesian people.' Howard's phrasing was somewhat hackneyed, borrowed perhaps from *Clichés for World Leaders: A Lexicon*, a book which has yet to be published but of which far too many people appear to have a copy. He was right to make the point, however. Choose words that emphasise that your criticism is of the Government, not of the nation. In this case, therefore, an improvement on 'The agreement was destroyed by French duplicity' would be:

Responsibility for the failure of this deal rests with the French Government.

In addition to the replacement of the overly broad phrase 'the French' with the more focussed 'the French Government', the tone of the line has changed. You are not suggesting that this behaviour is typical, and you don't sound as though you were *looking* for the French Government to fail. You are disappointed rather than angry, matter-of-fact rather than hysterical, and completely without xenophobia. This version too can be improved, however. At the moment, your statement that the French Government was to blame sounds like a *claim*. How can you make it sound like a fact? By changing your choice of words.

A *claim* is a suggested causal link or a reason that something happened. ('The French Government destroyed the agreement.') If, however, you merely *comment* on a causal link or claim, then your listeners' attention is focussed on your comment and not on the causal link itself. In essence, the claim has been taken as a solid, proven assertion. So, instead of claiming that 'Responsibility for the failure of this deal rests with the French Government', we could instead *use that claim as a basis for making a further comment.*

To see how that might be done, let us return once again to that East Timor speech by Australian PM John Howard. He *could* have said:

Indonesian forces totally failed to control the violence.

But he didn't. He didn't say that because that would have focussed questioning on whether or not the Indonesians *did* completely fail. It would have sounded like a *claim*. So he tried to make it sound more like a *fact*:

The total failure of the Indonesian forces to control the violence has greatly distressed the Australian people.

The link now being focussed on was whether or not the Indonesians' failure caused distress – and *not* whether or not the Indonesians really failed. Their failure had become a 'fact'.

Let's now see how we can make our claim that the French Government wrecked the deal sound less like a claim and more like a fact:

I think people throughout Europe will be disappointed by the French Government's failure to stick to the deal.

Now that the French Government has decided to collapse this deal, serious questions need to be asked about how we can make sure this does not happen again.

Despite the French Government's actions in bringing about the end of this deal, there is little to be gained from recriminations. Next week, if they will join us, we will be back at the negotiating table. We hope they do.

If this type of phraseology sounds familiar, it is because governments and political parties use it all the time. Merely by altering their choice of words, they are able to win people round to arguments which, if expressed differently, might have been much less effective.

This is not, we should stress, about 'brainwashing'. As with speech presentation, this is not a process for removing the importance of honesty and good argument. It is a process which complements good argument, and which can be *undermined* by dishonesty. The truth about language choice is much less dramatic than the conspiracy theorists would have us believe, but it is also much more complex and important than many speakers appreciate. Effective language choice cannot usually blind people, but it can help you to put across your case. Language which is clear, which supports your argument, and which sends out the right signals about *you* is vital to the art of persuasion. When your mother told you to mind your language, she was right.

5. SUMMARY

- **Language is important.** It affects your ability to convince people of your argument.

- **Choose language that is clear.** Clear language is free of jargon and made of words that people understand.

- **Choose language that supports your argument.** Words have resonances. Ask yourself what is the worst possible way that the words of your speech could be construed. Are there neighbouring words that might 'interfere' with your message?

- **Choose language that sends out the right signals about you.** Avoid language that might offend, or that might make it easy for opponents to stereotype you.

WRITING IT DOWN

1. THE NEED FOR A RESPONSIVE STYLE

There is a common misconception that a speech is a monologue. It is not: it's a conversation. Although only one party is able to communicate in detail, the other parties make their opinions known through interruptions, laughter, applause, silence and other forms of non-verbal expression. It is not always easy to sense exactly what the audience is communicating, but the more you watch and listen to them, the better your idea will be.

While you should never let an audience wrest control of your speech, it is important to try to respond to them. This does not necessarily require that you reply to illegitimate interruptions – what, in the British Parliament, are delicately called 'remarks made from a sedentary position' – but it does require that you build on the mood of the audience and the tone of the event. Audiences like to feel that you are talking *with* them rather than *to* them, and certainly not *at* them. This elevates the status of audience members to that of participants in a discussion rather than recipients of a top-down lecture, and reinforces their sense that you and they are on the same side. It also heightens their sense of responsibility to listen to what you are saying. Speakers who appear to be running counter to the responses of the audience can appear confrontational, while speakers who appear not to have noticed the audience can seem to be in another conversation altogether – with themselves perhaps, or their papers, or the back wall at which, for some reason, they have chosen to look rather than their audience.

Even if you read your speech out word for word, varying your tone will make you look less pre-primed and more frank. In general, however, it is almost always more effective not to read out your speech verbatim, but instead to use brief notes.

2. WHY USING NOTES WORKS

A *full* written text will constrain your speaking style – your attention and eye contact will be focussed on the text, rather than the audience. Opportunities for spontaneity and for responding to the audience will be quashed. Using *brief* notes, however, allows you to look at your audience rather than remaining glued to your papers; enables you to cut out the least important sections easily if you find yourself running out of time; and allows you to respond to points made by others much more easily. It also helps concentrate the mind, and reminds you of the core message you wish to get across.

There are, of course, times when a full written text may be appropriate. Earl Spencer's famous eulogy at the funeral of Princess Diana came across with such power and sincerity partly because it was read out with so much precision and so little showmanship. Speeches whose main importance is for public record and not persuasion – the setting out of a country's position at a UN security council meeting, for example – may also be best read out from a full text. The final text will probably be the result of negotiations between a multitude of different groups, and a small deviation could be considered a betrayal. Such exceptions do not undermine the general principle, however, and it is our experience that speakers rely on a full text far more often than they should.

If speaking from a full written text is inadvisable, how about the other extreme – speaking without notes at all? Speakers usually do this to sound more 'real', but it is in fact likely to have the opposite effect. If you speak completely extemporaneously, you are liable to ramble on without stopping. If you try to memorise a speech in its entirety, it takes so much effort that it becomes difficult to edit it on the day, or respond to the audience, without losing your way. It can make you less convincing, too. A witness who appeared not to be responding to the mood of the court but was instead trying to remember what to say would be less likely to convince a jury than one who appeared more conversational. Similarly, an unresponsive public speaker is a less credible public speaker.

Audiences have very little problem with a speaker using notes, as long as it doesn't prevent eye-contact. For the speakers themselves, notes can be so useful that the costs of getting rid of them far outweigh any benefits. Most great speakers use brief notes to guide the course of their speech. The notes President John F. Kennedy used when delivering his famous 'Ich bin ein Berliner' address, for example, are available for all to see at the *Haus der Geschichte* museum in Bonn. The notes consist of just the key concepts and phrases that he wanted to get across. Thus, the phrase 'Ich bin ein Berliner' is written phonetically in a long red scrawl across the notes.* If you've spent time planning your speech and thinking about its content, then a few key written phrases are all you are likely to need to trigger the different sections. The box below sets out one example of a good set of speech notes.

Speech to St Mary's School

Introduction:	Nice to be back. Thank you Headmaster. And I remember just how uncomfortable those seats you're sitting in are . . .
Background:	• At school 1975–1980.
	• Some teachers still here – like . . . (talk about Mr Melluish)
	• I got into trouble twice – explain why
Today:	• Run a business – explain what we do and how it affects young people
	[slide 1: local football team visiting the factory.]

---

*Kennedy's speech was given to show American commitment to West Berlin during the Cold War. The phrase Kennedy should have used – 'Ich bin Berliner' – means 'I am a Berliner.' What he actually said – 'Ich bin *ein* Berliner' – translates as 'I am a doughnut'. Nobody's perfect.

| Future: | • Why important to do exams: future regrets vs. future prospects.
• Post-exam feelings: worry if you haven't worked, relief if you have.
• What film stars have said about the importance of hard work.
[slide 2: Leonardo DiCaprio learning Shakespeare as a schoolboy.] |
| Summary: | • Good school. Don't waste it.
• Plan your day – you can work *and* play football – you just need to time your breaks. |

Depending on the duration of the anecdotes alluded to in the notes, the speech outlined might last anything between five and thirty minutes. To read the words on the page, however, takes only a matter of seconds. Thus, the speaker is free to concentrate on the audience but has the notes there as a guide. As you can see, the notes also guide the *structure* of the speech. When written on one large piece of paper,* the speaker has an overall plan view of the speech. The notes instantly convey that there are three sections – school background, position today and advice for the future. The notes therefore also serve as a map to make the context of each point immediately obvious. Such *visible structure* in your notes will make your speech more structured and easier to follow. Other systems, like using a series of small 'speech cards', don't provide this visible structure as effectively. They may be handy to hold, but they don't show how your speech fits together, and they don't give the flexibility of time and detail that having it all on one sheet does.

It is also worth noting that certain parts of the speech might be written out in complete sentences – most notably the

---

*A good tip is to use a heavy grade of paper. Many speakers find that, after folding up their notes to fit in their pocket and after unfolding them with sweaty hands, their notes are unreadable and crumpled. Better quality paper minimises this risk.

beginning and the end. As explained on pages 44 and 50, the opening and the conclusion of the speech are critical times. Many speakers like to write the first few sentences in full so as to 'settle' themselves during the nervous first few seconds of a speech. Similarly, many speakers like to write the last few sentences out in full in order to be sure to make their conclusion clear. The rest of the speech, however, works best from brief notes.

3. SUMMARY

- **A speech is not a monologue.** It is a conversation.

- **Working from brief notes allows speakers to be responsive and spontaneous, while still staying on track.** A full script or memorisation is too constraining. Impromptu talks can be too rambling. Brief notes put the speaker firmly in control.

- **The appearance of the written speech is important.** The structure of your speech should be apparent from the notes. You might want to write especially important sections (such as the introduction and conclusion) in full.

PRESENTING A SUCCESSFUL SPEECH

EVENT MANAGEMENT
SPEAKING IN A TECHNOLOGICAL AGE

EVENT MANAGEMENT

As we noted earlier, the audience's perception of a speech is influenced as much by presentation as it is by content. On pages 15 to 24 we looked at the fundamentals of presentation: confidence, respecting the audience and knowing the limits. There are, however, other issues. In the sketch we quoted about the Prime Minister's television broadcast, the clothes and background were almost as important as the Prime Minister himself (see page 15). The music, dress and aesthetics of a traditional Roman Catholic or High Anglican church service are strong reinforcers of the ideas of authority and timelessness. Likewise, the facing of all mosques to Mecca, the layout of courtrooms and the design of many other buildings all serve to impress a desired frame of mind on the inhabitants. Hence, the best public speakers don't just think about their own manner during their speech, they try to gear the whole event towards getting their message across. Here we outline some issues to consider in planning your event. Chief among them are:

- Organising the venue
- Image
- Involving the audience
- Managing expectations.

1. ORGANISING THE VENUE

GETTING THE TIME RIGHT

Timing is at least as important as location. Choose a time of day when people are alert. The box opposite offers a rough picture of people's alertness in a typical working day.

The dip in the graph reflects the fact that the bodies of the audience (and the speaker) are more concerned about digesting

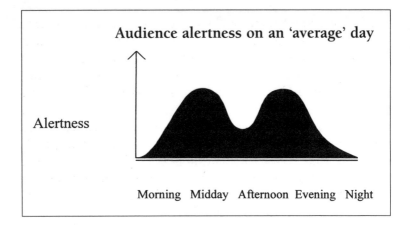

lunch than they are about keeping the senses alert. The best times to deliver your speech, therefore, are usually the hours *before* lunch or dinner – when people are most attentive.

CHOOSING THE RIGHT VENUE

As outlined above, choose a venue that breeds alertness and familiarity: you do not want the audience to snooze while you speak. A properly lit and well-ventilated room is of crucial importance in keeping your audience alert and attentive.

The type of venue that you choose will be interpreted by audience members as saying something about your message. A speech at a school or a community centre clearly evokes different images in the minds of listeners from a speech at a hotel. A company boss who wants to encourage employees to suggest radical new ideas will usually find that an event outside the confines of the workplace is more successful. No longer 'in work', people will feel more relaxed about speaking openly, and less constrained by day-to-day hierarchies.

Even if you are unable to choose the venue, you may be able to *arrange* the venue, planning where you will speak from, where you will be when you are not speaking and what your background will be. When British Prime Minister Tony Blair gave a speech in support of a 'Yes' vote on the Northern Ireland peace agreement, he stood in front of enlargements of promises he had written in his own handwriting. The message was that the promises were not just talk. Doubters often say 'I want that in writing,' and Blair's set was a response *par excellence* to this common cry. If you are speaking in aid of a charitable organisation, a large photograph that represents the people you help will provide a strong reinforcer, helping you to take people 'into the field'. If you are speaking to members of your trade union, business group or company, you may want to have your core message written in a slogan behind you. At the very least, make sure the background is not unnecessarily distracting. A table of people sitting behind you can do nothing but harm your authority. At best, you appear less important than the people who sit on the stage in order to look distinguished. At worst, audience members start watching the reactions of the people behind you, who may be talking to each other and/or falling asleep. If you can't get the attention-seekers off the stage, try to arrange for a single spotlight that leaves them in the dark, or break the rules by coming down off the stage and talking to the audience from the floor.

Get as close as you can to the audience. A small room where the speaker is close to the audience invariably makes for a better-received speech. The audience feel less able to 'switch off', for fear of being spotted by the speaker. Similarly, applause and cheers are always more infectious with a crowd that are close together, rather than a widely dispersed group of individuals. The debating chambers of the Oxford Union and the House of Commons are both arranged for the speakers to be able to look into their opponents' eyes. This provides for electrifying debates with lively audience response.

Check what equipment is available. Assume nothing. There is no point coming to give a speech that revolves around a video or a set of slides if they are then unshowable. Audience members sit bored while the organisers go running around the room looking for a video player or a slide projector, and are only cheered up by the *schadenfreude* of watching the completely undignified spectacle of a speaker struggling to put the right leads in the right sockets. As we outline in the next chapter (pages 133–42), technology has its uses, but two pieces of advice could save you a lot of pain and embarrassment: firstly, make sure the event organisers know what equipment you need; secondly, don't rely on them. Make sure you can deliver your speech even if they let you down.

2. IMAGE

The way you dress is one of the most important non-verbal signals that the audience will pick up. If you don't dress like a figure of authority, it will be more difficult to be regarded as one. Likewise, if you dress 'down' to an occasion which audience members consider important, they may well feel snubbed.

Even if those to whom you are speaking are themselves dressed informally, they may well expect you to be smarter – after all, you *are* the speaker. Audiences at Republican Party conventions in the USA, for example, are famous for their extraordinarily garish outfits designed to display their passionate partisanship. All the key speakers, however, wear suits. They don't dress like their audience, and their audience wouldn't want them to.

There is a reason why most politicians wear suits. The reason is that most politicians who don't wear suits don't get elected. There are, of course, famous exceptions, but the fact they are famous is testament to their scarcity. The Darwinian brutality of the ballot box has made this point clear in contests around the world. Most effective speakers have taken it on board. Think, for example, of the spokespeople of environmental pressure groups, who always wear suits when they appear on television because they know that, however impeccable their scientific argument, they would find it much more difficult to win people over to their case if they dressed like eco-warriors. Think of the militant left-wingers, committed to the overthrow of the class-system, who wear suits to party meetings because they need to look like leaders. Derek Hatton, leader of the Militant socialist council that ran Liverpool in the 1980s, dismissed the 'casual look' of middle-class liberals as offensive to working-class voters. If working for the people of Liverpool was an important job, he argued, he had to dress like it was an important job.

The importance of your appearance can be startling. In 1963 Stanley Milgram conducted a controversial series of experiments where he asked questions to a person ('the learner'), and if they answered incorrectly, they would receive an electric shock. The electric shocks were administered by ordinary members of the public who had volunteered to help, and who were instructed to increase the level of electric shock each time the learner got a question wrong. However, unbeknown to the volunteers, the learner was in fact an actor and didn't really receive an electric shock, but just *pretended* to scream in agony. Milgram found that, dressed as an authoritative scientist, he could persuade most volunteers to actually administer 'lethal' levels of electric shock if he instructed them to. However, when he repeated his experiments in a shabby set of offices and dressed less authoritatively, his influence over the volunteers was vastly diminished and far fewer of them administered high levels of shock. Your image, it seems, is very important.[1]

Not everyone agrees about the importance of respectable attire, and many have sought to win support to their cause through colourful outfits and a defiant refusal to dress like the 'establishment'. CND, the Campaign for Nuclear Disarmament, was one such organisation. In a book that captures the despair of more realistic activists at such tactics, former CND supporter John O'Farrell laments their failure to win over hearts and minds:

Somewhere between the 1960s and the 1980s CND must have hired the worst PR consultants in the world. The *Daily Mail* called the Greenham [protesters] 'woolly heads in woolly hats' – a jibe that struck a chord with the millions of people who were not used to having their arguments on defence strategy put to them by people in clown costumes. In the blackest days of the Second World War, when Churchill said 'If we fail, then civilisation will be thrown back into the Dark Ages', the country knew what he meant. The seriousness of his message would not have been particularly helped by his then putting on a luminous skeleton costume and throwing himself to the floor by means of illustration.[2]

Just as voters expect their political leaders to *dress* like leaders, audiences expect speakers to dress in a manner that reflects the importance of the event and the speaker's authority and expertise. This is not to say that you must always wear a suit, and is certainly not to prescribe any particular style: public speaking is not a fashion show. It is simply to recommend that you ask yourself, for each occasion, what style of dress will best indicate to your audience that you are a person worth listening to. At some occasions there will be a formal dress code, which it is usually best to follow. This is in your self-interest, because it puts you on good terms with your audience. Even if there is no formal dress code, however, the audience will draw conclusions about you from your clothes, conclusions which will influence their evaluation of your argument and their decision as to whether or not they agree with you. It is important, therefore, to dress in a way which shows – not just to the most supportive members of the audience but also to the most suspicious – that you respect yourself and that you respect them.

3. INVOLVING YOUR AUDIENCE

THE 'NOT JUST WORDS' APPROACH

An audience whom you actively involve in your speech is much more likely to remember and be persuaded by it than an audience you relegate to being mere listeners. This relates to the way that human beings think. Public speaking expert Dale Carnegie put it starkly:

> People are not thinking about you or me or caring what is said about us. They are thinking about themselves – before breakfast, after breakfast, and right on until ten minutes past midnight. They would be a thousand times more concerned about a slight headache of their own than they would about the news of your death or mine.[3]

Inviting the audience to actively help you improves their memory of your speech, because people generally remember things that *they* did themselves more than they remember things others told them. The tourist leaving the museum remembers the exact wording of his comments in the visitors' book at least as well as he remembers the museum itself – just as the audience member recalls his own actions better than your words.

In *Easily Led*, a brilliant examination of propaganda, historian Oliver Thomson notes:

> Audience participation is a recognised aid to educational learning – also valuable in propaganda. Organising crowds to shout slogans, carry banners, sing campaign songs, repeat the propaganda message in some form or another makes conversion more likely . . . Requests for fairly small acts of compliance . . . become the psychological foot-in-the-door for acceptance of the whole ideology . . . An audience involved can be more tractable than an audience allowed to become totally passive.[4]

Irish Nationalist Michael Collins used to ask his audience: 'If they take me, *who* will replace me?' If his listeners remembered nothing else about the speech, you can bet they remembered how they felt when they shouted back 'I will!' American Evangelist Billy Graham calls upon individual audience members to come down to the stage. Anyone that has ever happened to can usually remember it. You don't need to be a religious leader or a nationalist firebrand to make use of such techniques. One suggestion is as follows.

Invite your audience to complete a simple task after your talk. Sometimes this is just a matter of course – for example, you may ask other members of a board to vote with you at the end of a meeting, or you may be speaking at a campaign rally and ask the audience for donations. However, even if there is no *technical need* for action on the part of the audience, it is sometimes a good idea to devise a task for them to do.

There is, nonetheless, an art to devising appropriate tasks for your audience to perform. The task should be completed right after the end of your speech – when the audience is still buoyed-up by your words and stirred by your arguments. It should also be simple enough not to require any substantial effort, but personal enough to leave a lasting impression. Here are some sample scenarios:

- *Following a speech about the injustice of a particular law*: distribute pre-written postcards to the audience and ask them to sign them and post them to their local MP.
- *Following a seminar*: ask the audience to write down their e-mail addresses and hand them to you, so that you can send them some supplementary information.
- *Following a speech to employees about improving efficiency*: ask each person to fill in a form there and then suggesting a simple way things could be improved. Promise to reply to them – and make sure you do.

We should, perhaps, add a final note of caution. If, following your speech, you plan to appeal for *financial* assistance from the audience, it is usually best not to sound like you are making demands. That is not to say that you shouldn't explain exactly how their individual donations will count, but it is to say that you should avoiding appearing like a speaker obsessed by donations and money. The 'Not Just Words' approach is about getting the audience to feel sympathetic to your cause, and badgering them for money is a sure way to destroy their sympathy.

Getting your audience to take part in the event will greatly improve the impact of your message. At the very least, speakers should make time for audience members to participate through questions, as set out below.

ANSWER QUESTIONS WITH RESPECT

When answering questions posed by Opposition Members in the British House of Commons, the Prime Minister's aim is not to win over the minds of the questioners. Neither the questioner nor the questioned treats the debate as a genuine discussion; it is, instead, a rhetorical point-scoring exercise. Both sides aim merely to catch their opponents out and humiliate them in front of the cameras. Most question and answer sessions are not like that, however. Usually, you *do* want to get your questioners to agree with you. It is advisable, therefore, to answer their questions with respect.

Some questions might be very salient. Others may well be ridiculous but, if you decide to point that out, the questioner is likely to feel that you consider him a ridiculous *person*. With his own pride at stake, the questioner is unlikely to yield completely or graciously. It is usually better, therefore to facilitate a more positive, friendly and 'engaged' dialogue with the questioner, by beginning your reply with a phrase like 'I see what you mean . . .' or 'Yes, that's a good question but . . .' Likewise, if someone asks you a hostile question, it is generally better not to snap back or look rattled but to try, instead, to be more reasonable than the questioner. Whatever you do, avoid abusing questioners: it is unfair to expect them to be as well versed on your chosen topic as you are, and abusive or abrupt responses do little to win the audience's respect. If the question really is stupid, it shouldn't be difficult to deal with: 'Several people have expressed that point of view but the evidence seems largely to point in the other direction . . .'; 'That's an interesting question, and it's not one to be dismissed lightly, but I think in the end I'd have to disagree with you. Let me try to persuade you . . .'. This doesn't stop you from being able to explain to the audience why the questioner is wrong. In fact, it makes it much easier, and at least allows you the possibility of winning over the person who asked the question.

RESPOND IN DETAIL TO YOUR AUDIENCE'S QUESTIONS
There are two main schools of thought about how you should answer your audience's questions. One says that you should always tackle them head-on. Another says you should not. The second school should not be dismissed simply as liars and snake-oil salesmen. There is a perfectly legitimate argument in their favour: answering a question directly, they say, serves to keep the discussion within the framework set by the questioner – a framework which is at best irrelevant and at worst hostile. Instead, they contend, you should try to shift the discussion back into *your* framework. Whatever the questioner asks, they suggest, respond in a way which reinforces your point rather than answering theirs. This argument is, as we said, perfectly legitimate. It is also, however, wrong.

The 'dodge the question' approach is wrong for two reasons. Firstly, it makes the speaker look shifty. Even the most eloquent and erudite response will not acquit speakers who fail to actually answer the question. The audience's reaction? 'Yeah, he's really clever. Had all the right responses up his sleeve. Didn't answer anyone's questions, though. Wouldn't trust him further than I could throw him.'

The second reason is that it is unnecessary. There is no need to make a choice as to whether you give a direct answer or shift the discussion back into your framework. In fact, you can do both. You 'have the floor' and determine the length of your answers. This makes it quite possible to spend twenty or thirty seconds answering the question within the parameters set by the questioner – thereby proving your willingness to answer the question – and then say something like 'Well, that's the short answer to your question, but actually you've raised another, perhaps more important, point there and I'd like to try to deal with that too . . .'. At that point you can move the discussion into the place you feel it should be happening, and you will be seen to have advanced the argument rather than to have retreated from it.

This applies even if you are asked a question to which you don't know the answer or which appears to undermine your argument. Instead of rejecting your questioner's point outright, thank her for bringing the new information to your attention, and then explain why your argument still holds. 'That's an interesting example, and it's one of the best I've heard on your side of the argument, but I think my point still stands . . .'; 'Let's suppose that everything in that example is exactly as you describe it – and I don't know whether it is or not. But you seem to have researched this matter in considerable depth, so let's suppose it is. I still think, even then, that my point holds true. This is because . . .'; 'Well I haven't heard that particular example but there are anecdotes that illustrate both sides of the argument [briefly list some examples to prove you're not bluffing]. The important point, though, is that . . .' No one can accuse you of having avoided the question, since you have dealt with it head-on. Neither, however, have you allowed the discussion to be 'hijacked'. The issues raised by the questioner have been dealt with, but the issues raised in your speech remain central.

SPECIAL POINTS TO NOTE ABOUT DEBATES

No complete guide to public speaking can ignore debating – which is, after all, what the Oxford Union is best known for. Debating has its own peculiarities about how questions should be asked and responded to, and may not be familiar to everyone. It is, however, increasingly popular, and all speakers would do well to master the essentials.

As is clear from the rules of debating given in the appendix, a speaker in a debate is usually only allowed to speak for a few minutes. During his or her speech, audience members and opposition debaters are allowed to stand up and say 'point of information'. (A point of information is a short, relevant interruption – perhaps a comment or a question – which attempts to refute or weaken the speaker's argument.) The speaker can choose whether to pause and hear the point, or may simply decline the interruption. There is, however, an art both to offering and accepting points of information.

The art to making them is to keep them short – no more than a matter of seconds. A short, snappy, point leaves the speaker no time to think of a clever (or any) response. If the questioner makes their point quickly, then the onus is on the speaker to fill up the silence by answering the point. Short, concise points can therefore be deadly.

The art of dealing with them is to control *when* you allow yourself to be interrupted. You, as the speaker, have control of the floor. You should therefore have no qualms about only accepting interruptions that are concerned with your 'best' points. That way, your opponents are restricted to attacking you on your most solid ground. If part of your speech involves, for example, making an unpopular point (such as 'We may not like the thought of criminals going unpunished, but our justice system has to be fair'), then you can bet that you'll receive a swarm of points of information during that phase of your speech. You can also bet that the audience will find it easy to applaud someone who attacks your unpopular points. It is safest, therefore, to limit interruptions to the best sections of your speech.

It is also important to demonstrate that you are in control of the floor. A speaker truly in control will finish the point they are making before they let someone interrupt.

The final tactical element in accepting points of information concerns the *amount* of interruptions you allow. If you allow none, you can look like you are afraid to be challenged. If you allow more than one interruption every couple of minutes, you might be in danger of letting your speech be controlled by the audience. However, there is one type of speech where you should be keen to allow interruptions. The person speaking first in a debate – or, for that matter, the first speaker of the day at a conference – has no 'atmosphere' to play off. The first speaker then has an uphill struggle to inject some life into the proceedings and to make things seem contentious and exciting. Allowing more interruptions is then a good way of making the speech seem more responsive, more lively and more spontaneous.

The importance of points of information is that they provide a mini-battle within the speech. A speaker who responds to a good point with a phrase like 'Yes, I accept that', 'No, that's not true' or the ubiquitous 'I'll deal with that later' will look less credible. Giving witty, sharp and informed responses to points of information is a hallmark of the best speakers. Next time you watch a speaker in a debate who's 'on a roll', just note how few people stand up to challenge her with points of information.

4. MANAGING EXPECTATIONS

Under-hype an event and no one turns up. Over-hype it and audiences arrive expecting too much. The expectation is always greater than the realisation. An audience unaware that they are about to hear a great speech are always more grateful than those who went along expecting one. How, without over-hyping it, can you get audiences to come? One way, used by conference organisers, is to 'bribe' participants with a week of fun. (A rule of thumb: the nicer the conference resort, the duller the speakers.) This is not always possible, however, and even when it is possible it will often just bring the participants to the conference, and not to the actual auditorium. A better suggestion is to promote your talk as being important, rather than being entertaining or erudite: this will be the speech where you reveal your new policy or your new product, or the speech where you explain how people can join your organisation. The audience will turn up of their own accord because they feel they need to. Any brilliance in your speech will count as a bonus.

5. SUMMARY

- **Organise a venue that reinforces your message**. And hold your meeting at a time when people are most alert.

- **What you wear is one of the most important non-verbal signals you send out.** Dress in a way that suggests you are someone to take seriously.

- **Involve your audience.** The 'Not Just Words' approach can help to make your speech more memorable and entrench any impact that your speech makes.

- **Answer questions properly.** Treat your questioners with respect, and don't dodge their questions.

- **If you take part in a debate, take enough points of information to allow you to show spontaneity and confidence in your argument.** (But don't take so many that you lose your argumentative flow.)

- **Manage expectations.** Let people know that your speech is important, but don't promise them the world, or it will be hard to exceed what people expected.

SPEAKING IN A TECHNOLOGICAL AGE

In ancient times, public speaking was largely a matter of shouting loudly enough, so that as many people could hear you as possible. Sometimes, those nearer the front of the crowd would repeat the speaker's words to those standing further back, and the message would be disseminated along a chain of whispers. These days things are a bit more hi-tech. In this section, we will examine the strengths and weaknesses of each audio-visual aid, and how to use them with success. To this end, we will look at:

- The basic principles of using audio-visual aids.
- Static visual aids.
- Dynamic audio-visual aids.
- Why gadgets aren't everything.

1. PRINCIPLES
Fewer and fewer people are used to listening to long, unbroken speeches devoid of any sort of technological accompaniment. Some purists wail that this is a sad state of affairs, and long for a return to the 'great age of oratory'. (The 'great age of oratory' always being just a generation before the current one.) However, the changes technology has made to speechmaking should be welcomed. Science and technology define the age we currently live in – they have had beneficial effects on our health, our standard of living, our productivity and our understanding of other cultures. Why should technology not also have had a beneficial effect on public speaking? The answer is that it has, and in two distinct ways.

The reason that news broadcasts contain speech interspersed with clips and interviews (rather than just pure speech) is not that the producers of these programmes have an aversion to untampered oratory. The simple fact is that news delivered in this manner is more exciting and more informative. Cutting between news anchorman and video clips stimulates the senses. There is variety, diversity and it holds the attention well. It is not only more enjoyable, but it maintains concentration for longer and is therefore more effective. Some professions seem reluctant to embrace a similar style of presentation – too many sermons or lectures, for example, are delivered as half-hour orations. How much more effectively could religious leaders or lecturers convey their points if they were prepared to use video clips or computer graphics to illustrate their point? Traditionalists might well complain at such innovations, but traditionalists would also be more able to understand your speech because of those innovations.

The other benefit of audio-visual aids is that pictures are a keenly effective method of making your point. A television or video clip presents information and lets the viewer form their own conclusions. Viewers feel more able to accept facts that they see with their own eyes, rather than being persuaded of the facts by a speaker: they feel as though they are making up their own mind. Anyone who doubts the importance of visual images just needs to look at the way in which TV pictures undermined the American public's support for the Vietnam War. Images are powerful tools of persuasion. As the saying goes, 'I know it's true, I saw it with my own eyes'.

Given that visual images are a powerful source of persuasion and interest, let's consider some general tips for how to successfully integrate audio-visual technology into a speech.

- *Don't let a power cut ruin your speech.* Be prepared in case the technology fails – either by thinking of another way to show the images, or just by being prepared, if necessary, to talk without the technological aid.
- *Don't waste the entertainment value of the audio-visuals.* Audiences normally welcome the use of audio-visual displays, as

they provide variety in a talk. Long, unedited sequences of video or slides can destroy the novelty value. It is unimaginably easy for the audience to drift off to sleep when the lights are dimmed for a protracted period.

- *Use the technology with purpose.* Visual images are normally best used to provide an overall picture of the talk (for example, a handout that clarifies the main points of your talk) or to highlight specific examples (for example, by showing short video clips). However, *purposeless* visual displays (for example, using slides containing dense text as a substitute for lecture notes) serve only to distract the audience.

2. STATIC VISUALS

BLACKBOARDS AND FLIP CHARTS

Technologically backward it may be, but the blackboard has deservedly remained a centrepiece of classroom teaching for decades. Blackboards and flip charts are ideal aids to use when seeking to *educate* an audience. They serve as a useful control on the speaker's pace – as the time needed to note down a point far exceeds the time needed to say it. A realistic pace for note-giving encourages the audience to jot down the material and thus *engages* them in the act of learning. Good blackboard work requires the speaker to follow only a few simple principles:

- *To gain variety, it is often best to explain concepts verbally, and then note down the important points on the blackboard.* This encourages the audience to halt their furious note-taking and listen. You are a more powerful persuader in person than your writing is on the blackboard.
- *Engage your audience all the time.* Try to keep at least part of your face visible as you write. Make sure you talk as you note points on the board. This all ensures that the atmosphere is kept alive and provides an excellent chance to re-emphasise

your main points. Repetition, as we saw earlier, is the key to spreading your message.

- *Try dividing the blackboard into two unequal portions.* Use the smaller half to note down the outline of your talk – as this will enable the audience to 'see' where the talk is heading and imparts a sense of *context* to your points. (See the 'wood for the trees' principle on page 58–60.)

SLIDES, *POWERPOINT* AND OVERHEAD PROJECTORS

Slides, *Powerpoint*-style packages and overhead projectors are the favourite toys of speakers at seminars. They allow *real* data or information to be shown, rather than just the rough sketch that a blackboard requires. Because they provide a means of enticing the audience through visual images, they are often referred to as oratory's equivalent of a dessert trolley. They are, however, frequently over-used – especially when speakers plan their speech around the images, using text on the overheads as a substitute for lecture notes. It is often best, therefore, to use slides or overheads to demonstrate *examples*, and move to a blackboard when wishing to note down key points. The main tips for successfully using projectors are:

- *Check the sequence of the transparencies in advance.* If you need to show the same transparency twice, then produce two copies – this is far more professional than winding the slide projector back to the relevant slide.
- *Each slide or acetate should highlight one concept.* A frame that contains multiple points detracts from your speech.
- *The images need to be simple, so remove unnecessary words or pictures.* Many speakers make the mistake of simply photo-copying a page of a book or a journal on to a transparency. Figures contained in print are often cramped for spatial reasons and contain extra information that the reader can refer back to at leisure. In those respects, unedited figures lifted from a printed medium are *not* ideal for use in your talk.

- *Text must be clearly visible*. As a rule of thumb, there should be less than ten lines of text per transparency. The text on an A4-size transparency should therefore be at least 1 cm in height.
- *Don't overdo the number of frames*. If you've got more than about one frame for every two minutes of speech, then you've probably got too many.

Figures 3 and 4 show some examples of well-designed and shabbily designed transparencies.

3. DYNAMIC AUDIO-VISUALS

VIDEOS AND COMPUTER GRAPHICS

Video and computer-generated movies are a great way of holding audience interest, especially when addressing younger audiences. They are an ideal method for partitioning a long speech into manageable sections. In that respect, they are useful for lectures, seminars and even after-dinner speeches. Following a short movie clip, the audience feels refreshed and ready to listen to another small section of speech.

Video and computer projectors are a vastly under-used resource. The cost of the technology required becomes cheaper every year, and most venues should at least be able to provide a television and video recorder to accompany your talk – yet few speakers bother to use them. Speeches that do include video and computer technology therefore appear more innovative and their novelty value brings a healthy attention dividend. The key tips to note when using this type of technology include those previously described for slides (see page 136) as well as the extra ones below:

- *The sound, light and action of a video clip can easily overshadow your talk, so use the clips sparingly*. Your talk should be supported by the video, not the other way round. Similarly,

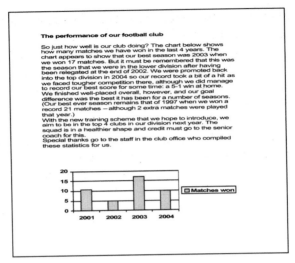

Figure 3: *This is a poor slide.* The text at the top of the slide not only distracts the audience's attention from the figure at the bottom (and from the speaker) but also uses so much space that the chart becomes illegible.

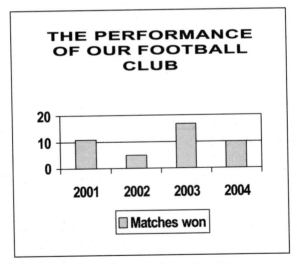

Figure 4: *This is a better slide.* The unnecessary text has been cropped as the speaker can supply this in their speech. This allows a larger font to be used so even the people at the back of the room can see the slide.

it is best to do the voice-overs 'live' if possible, rather than using the commentary from the video clip.

- *When not in use, the movie technology should not be a distraction.* Computer screensavers with little green men dancing over the screen or a muted (but running) video tape will draw attention *away* from your speech, however interesting it may be.

- *Prepare well in advance.* Order your computer sequences and edit your videotape so as to avoid constant fast-forwarding or rewinding. Check with your hosts that their equipment is compatible with your needs: for example, British videos use PAL format, whereas US machines use NTSC format. Test that everything works before the audience assemble for your talk.

MICROPHONES

Microphones can catch even the best speakers out. President Reagan was once asked to test the microphones before he delivered a crucial address. Joking, he stepped up to the microphone and said, 'I must tell the nation that our economy is in one hell of a mess.' However, the microphone had already been connected to various press offices and his words caused a ripple of panic. Stories abound of similar gaffes and unintentional amplification. It is always best, therefore, to assume that your microphone is on. People sitting on discussion panels should bear this advice in mind, for many microphone gaffes have been caused by a panel member muttering obscenities under their breath while smiling sweetly and vigorously nodding in agreement with the speaker. The key tips for successful microphone work are:

- *Don't feel you have to use one.* Most people speak more freely and with a more natural tone when they dispense with the microphone. Over-zealous hosts may well have provided rock-concert-like microphones and amplifiers, even if you are speaking to three rows of empty chairs in a village hall.

Unless you only have a tiny lung capacity, it is best to dispense with the mike in a situation like this, as it will make things seem more natural.

- *If you do use one, harness its range.* If you want to really emphasise a point, then just lean in slightly and let the microphone boom your words out. If you do this too much throughout the speech, the audience will become irritated with the constant loud noise. Used sparingly, however, it is a very powerful technique for highlighting selected sentences.

- *Most microphones (clip-on or hand-held) work best when held about twenty centimetres from the mouth (roughly the length between elbow and wrist).* At that distance, you should project your voice as though the microphone was absent. The distance between your mouth and the microphone ensures that unwanted breathing sounds aren't transmitted. These are commonly referred to as 'popping your "p"s', because of the air sound made when the lips push out a word that begins with the letter p.

- *Ask your host well in advance what type of microphones will be provided.* Clip-on microphones are often accompanied by a bulky transmitter box that you have to conceal in your clothing – a bulging square box jammed underneath a dress can look very inelegant. However, if you are likely also to be using, say, an overhead projector, you may want to request a clip-on mike so that your hands are free to manipulate the slides.

4. GADGETS AREN'T EVERYTHING

Changes in technology have provided a host of new ways to present one's case. Speakers can, for example, offer much more than just their words to back them up: they can show video-taped 'proof'. The progress of technology, however, seems to have created not a 'modern' people but a 'post-modern' people. People like technology, but they do not want to be controlled by it. They do not associate high-tech communication with sincerity, and they do not associate mass communication with emotional attachment. Company bosses who communicate to their employees with an annual video message can seem too slick and too distant. Even in the most technologically advanced societies, politicians still hold public meetings, shoppers are still entertained by street performers, and musicians still play live and, for ultimate credibility, unplugged. The 1999 blockbuster movie *The Blair Witch Project* enthralled the critics not *in spite* of the fact that it was so low-tech (total production budget: $30,000) but partly *because* it was so low-tech – so 'life-like'.

In the famous murder trial of O. J. Simpson in the USA, the prosecution offered (controversial) test results from high-tech research equipment. O. J. Simpson's low-tech response was to put on a replica of the glove worn by the murderer, and demonstrate that it didn't fit. How did his attorney successfully summarise the evidence to the jury? 'If the glove don't fit, acquit.'* American Evangelist Billy Graham's continuing success as a preacher has been put down by one analyst to his use of 'the latest advertising techniques, of music, of television, including satellite, *and of traditional revivalist preaching*'.[1] Speakers can benefit a great deal from mastering technology, but should never become slaves to gadgetry for gadgetry's sake. They can spread their message to many more people than before by engaging with the mass media, but should avoid becoming so entangled with it that they cease to meet face-to-face with those whom they seek to win over.

Technology does not win every battle, and rarely wins alone. As economist Paul Krugman remarks,

> It is all too easy to fall into a kind of facile 'mega-trends' style of thought in which the wonders of the new are cited

---

*The authors do not suggest that this is the sole explanation for the acquittal, an event that appears to have created a literary genre of its own. We use this example solely to note the limits of 'high-tech' persuasion. Please don't send us any letters.

and easy assumptions are made that everything is different now. Of course the world has changed – but it was a pretty remarkable place even before the coming of the large-scale integrated circuit.[2]

Krugman's advice should be borne in mind. The context of public speaking has changed, but the issues that have always surrounded public speaking have not gone away. Technology has provided useful tools for speakers, but the speech – what is said and how – is still key.

5. SUMMARY

- **Audio-visual technology is a tool, not a threat.** It stimulates interest and it helps to make your points clear.

- **Prepare thoroughly.** Put your slides in sequence, enquire about the nature and compatibility of the technology at the venue and have a plan in case the equipment fails.

- **Mix your audio-visual aids.** Blackboard for notes, transparencies for examples. All have different strengths and weaknesses. More variety creates more interest.

- **Make the visuals simple.** Remove unnecessary text and information. Use large, visible letters.

- **Video technology is powerful.** It has novelty value and creates great interest. Ensure, however, that it does not overshadow or distract from your speech.

- **Microphones present dangers.** Always assume they are on. If you have to use them, then project normally into them from a distance of about twenty centimetres.

- **Don't get obsessed by technology.** Technology has provided useful tools for speakers, but has not replaced the need for good argument and good oratory.

SPECIALIST SKILLS

SPEAKING THROUGH THE MEDIA
SPEAKING IN BUSINESS AND COMMITTEE MEETINGS
SPEAKING AT WEDDINGS

SPEAKING THROUGH THE MEDIA

The mass media offer speakers the chance to reach unprecedented numbers of people. In the conflict between the Soviet forces and the Afghan Mujahadeen in the 1980s, it was said that 'a radio transmitter was worth a thousand Kalashnikovs'.[1] When Nelson Mandela became President of South Africa in 1994, his inaugural speech could be addressed literally, and not just rhetorically, to people in every country of the world. Public speakers can gain much from the effective use of mass media, but to do so they have to learn new techniques and strategies. Two things are central: maximising the advantages of the media, and making sure the media don't take advantage of *you*.

1. MAXIMISING THE ADVANTAGES OF THE MEDIA

To get the most out of the media, you do not only need to be aware of all the general issues of presentation mentioned earlier (covered particularly in the chapters on 'The basics of presentation' and 'Event management'). You need to choose the media that can most help your cause, and you need also to be clued-up about three aspects particular to audiences watching your speech on TV: they see you much closer up, they pay even more attention to the visual image, and they observe you in the context of their home.

ALL MEDIA ARE NOT THE SAME

Many speakers blindly seize any opportunity to speak on TV or radio without considering who their speech will reach. Such speakers may be wasting their time. Some programmes are highly influential, others are largely irrelevant. As British MP Paul Flynn once said of an interview he took part in for an obscure hospital radio station: 'Many of the maximum of one hundred listeners were asleep, too infirm to remove their headphones or dead.'[2]

It is important to analyse not only how many people are likely to tune in to hear your speech, but also *which* people. Advertisers focus on this question every day when attempting to secure the slot in the viewing schedules that best captures their target consumers. Likewise, speakers should try to ensure they appear on the broadcasts that best reach their target audience. The expensive way to do this is to hire marketing consultants to get a more detailed picture of what programmes your target audience watch. Better value for money can be had simply by reading the figures in the trade press.

TV IMAGES ARE CLOSE-UP

In Ancient Greece, the essential element in public speaking was a powerful voice to make yourself heard in the open air – and it was said that the secret of Demosthenes' powerful oratory was that he practised his speeches by the sea, against the noise of crashing waves.[3] Television has changed all that. The TV image captures not just the speaker's voice, but also the smallest half-smile and facial twitch. Speakers communicating via television have to pay special attention to such issues of close-up presentation. Richard Nixon's heavy, sweaty TV image in the 1960 US presidential election debate famously contributed to Kennedy's election victory. (Though Nixon lost among TV viewers, it was said that he 'won' in the radio broadcast of the same debate. It didn't help much: the TV debate was the crucial one.) Delivering a speech in the TV age requires speakers to be 'switched on' to the images they are conveying.

The box overleaf gives some key tips for brushing up your appearance before facing the cameras. Such issues can seem vain and frivolous, but they *are* important. Most people think about their physical appearance when, for example, preparing for a job interview – because they know that first impressions matter. The first impression you give to a TV audience is just as important.

Two Things to Check Before Going on TV

It is normal that the TV crew may give you a hand with make-up for the camera. However, they won't fuss over you, so you need to check some things yourself:

- *Pick tele-friendly clothes.* Checks or narrow stripes can strobe on screen and seem psychedelic. Similarly, shiny rimmed spectacles reflect light away from the face and may make you look shifty.

- *Check your last-minute appearance.* For example, many men find that they need to shave again before appearing on TV as stubble looks heavier under studio lights – especially in comparison to an immaculately made-up interviewer. A skewed tie or smudged lipstick can also be easily corrected before going on air.

You're on display, and the smallest things will be picked up. It's therefore important to be aware of any quirky phrases that you are prone to using, or mannerisms – including those mannerisms you have when you are merely listening to others speak. Some speakers advise doing your least important interview first. A safer approach, however, is to practise with friends or colleagues and get them to offer candid and critical advice. Sharpen up *before* you face the cameras. Later, watch a video of your performance, and don't let pride prevent you from seeing what you could have done better. Only your opponents stand to gain from your never seeing what you need to improve.

VISUAL IMAGERY MATTERS MORE ON TV

The importance of visual image in televised events is an opportunity as well as a challenge. On page 120 we discussed how the visual backdrop to your speech has a profound effect on your image. When communicating via TV this is even more important. The press conference allows you to select a venue based entirely on its appearance. The numbers of people reached through the press makes investment in visual imagery worthwhile. The short time you have to get your message across makes it vital that you maximise the clarity and force of your argument if it is to be memorable and persuasive.

It is a cliché, but a true one, that a picture paints a thousand words. Background images can improve the clarity of your message and make it more interesting and more retainable. In crises, for example, politicians often use gardens as the backdrop for speeches: they help to convey an image of calm. In a brilliant party political broadcast produced by film maker David Puttnam, Neil Kinnock, then British Labour leader, was filmed talking about his childhood while walking around parts of South Wales, his home region. Viewers felt that it was not just the 'politician' talking (as would have been suggested by an office backdrop), but the 'real person'. The scenery served to reinforce the message of the speech.

One very effective approach used by policy makers is to invite people who will benefit from their proposal to come along to the press conference, and be filmed with the speaker. This helps to guide viewers' interpretations of the speech. British Deputy Prime Minister John Prescott, unveiling a new transport strategy to reduce car use, was filmed alongside a young asthma sufferer: attention was drawn to the 'positive' side of the proposal – helping asthma sufferers – and away from the 'negative' side – restrictions for car users.

There are no simple rules to follow when deciding on the visual imagery to use in televised presentations, but three questions may help to structure the decision-making process:

1. *Is it feasible?* This is not only a question of time or money, but also of laws and regulations. In a campaign to highlight the export of horses for meat, The Royal Society for the Prevention of Cruelty to Animals used an image of a pony

hung up on a butcher's hook. The Advertising Standards Authority issued advice to the media asking them not to repeat the advert because the event it depicted, though real, was unrepresentative and distasteful. The campaign had to be relaunched. Lesson? Ensure that your images will not land you in trouble.[4]

2. *Does the image reinforce or distract from the message?* During a major speech by British Chancellor Gordon Brown on policy towards the European single currency, the image in the background was a new board displaying share prices at the London stock exchange. The impression the Chancellor hoped to convey was one of modernity (the flashy electronic board) and fiscal orthodoxy (the stock exchange). On the day he gave the speech, however, share prices fell. As he spoke the screens behind him went red to indicate falling prices. The impression was of the world falling around him. Lesson? Take care that the image really does reinforce your point.

3. *Can it be done better?* President Clinton once had to make a speech in favour of a highly controversial bill to permit late abortions. His first instinct might have been to surround himself with senior doctors, to demonstrate scientific backing. In fact, such an approach would have been seen by many merely to represent the combined forces of the political and medical establishment, and would not have helped to overcome people's *moral* reservations. He therefore chose a more emotionally sensitive image, and surrounded himself with women who owed their lives to the procedure. One speech might not change anyone's mind, but Clinton realised that image was still important. Lesson? Don't just stick with the first idea that comes to mind. Always ask if you could be doing it better.

Visual imagery is a hugely powerful force. Used effectively, it can be a great reinforcer of your spoken message. Seeing might not quite equal believing, but it comes very close.

TV IMAGES ARE NORMALLY SEEN IN THE HOME

People watching a speech on the TV or listening to it on the radio do not react in the same way as people at a rally or in a hall. Even if a million people are listening to your speech, they are probably listening to it within the privacy of their home, and there may be at most only one or two other people present with them. The most effective TV and radio speeches, therefore, may not be those given in the style of an address to a large crowd, but those that seem more like a small discussion. US President Franklin D. Roosevelt's radio addresses in the 1930s were so effective because they resembled – and were even called – 'fireside chats'. In contrast, former British Labour leader Neil Kinnock, generally a very effective speaker, helped to scupper his chances of winning the 1992 general election by appearing at a mass rally in which he shouted, 'We're all right! We're all right!' to an ecstatic crowd. For those at the rally, such exuberance was very effective. For viewers watching a thirty-second clip from the calm of their own home it appeared over the top, immature at best, demagogic at worst. Kinnock temporarily forgot that his most important audience wasn't at the rally; they were at home watching television. Viewers usually want something more measured, more 'one-to-one', than the kind of speech that excitable crowds will enjoy. Tune your speech to reflect the needs of both audiences, and prioritise the one you consider more important.

2. DON'T LET THE MEDIA TAKE ADVANTAGE OF YOU

Stories of hostile news editing abound. Many celebrities have claimed that they have suffered from 'contextual editing'. They may be photographed at, for example, a tense moment in a tennis match. The picture will then be banked in an archive. When a story breaks about trouble in their home or professional life, the tennis players and the other spectators will be edited out of the picture, and, hey presto, the editors have a wonderful picture of a tense-looking celebrity to print next to their story. However, media editing does not always arise from venom. It is, instead, an inescapable part of news reporting. News stations would need much more than twenty-four hours to report and explain all that had happened in one day. They *have* to edit. In doing so, however, they necessarily distort reality. They focus on what is most dramatic, most exciting and most controversial. 'If one person in a crowd is hurt,' writes Edward De Bono, 'the cameras will, where possible, be on that person.'[5] However legitimate that is journalistically, it leaves viewers with a distorted picture of that event. The same applies to the reporting of your speech. The part of your speech most likely to be broadcast is the part when you said something controversial, or insensitive, or misinterpretable. After all, from a journalist's perspective, that's the biggest 'event' of your speech. You don't have to be a victim, however, and there are three main ways of preventing the media from manipulating your speech:

- Be careful with your language.
- Channel the media's attention.
- Don't be battered by interviewers.

BE CAREFUL WITH YOUR LANGUAGE
You need to choose your words so as to avoid *wilful misinterpretation*. When speaking through the media, just one sentence from your speech can become the whole communicated message. *You* no longer set the context for your speech, so all the parts of your speech must work well even when they 'stand alone'.* Two real-life examples illustrate the point.

In the 1988 US presidential elections, Democratic contender Michael Dukakis was taunted by Republican opponents for

---

*All the points made in our chapter on 'Language' apply also when speaking to the media. In fact, they are even more important than usual. Look back at the summary on page 109 if you need a reminder.

being a 'liberal'.* Initially, he denied the accusation. Later on, he tried to neutralise the issue with a redefinition of liberalism: 'If by liberal you mean somebody who is deeply committed to full employment, equal economic opportunity for every American, a decent education for every American, basic health care for every working family in this country and a decent retirement, then I'm a liberal.' Unsurprisingly, the media were much less interested in such definitional arguments and much more in the fact that he had 'admitted' something he had previously denied. On top of that, they had him on tape to prove it. Only the last three words of his explanation – 'I'm a liberal' – received any attention or comment: sometimes they were the only words of his speech that were broadcast. His message about building a decent society was lost and his opponents were able to have a field day with the story of his shock new 'admission'. A much more effective approach would have been for Dukakis to say something like:

> The Republicans are trying to win this by name-calling.
> Personally, I'm not interested in that kind of debate, and I
> don't think that the public are either. Let me instead say
> plainly what I believe in, and people can decide for
> themselves whether *they* want that kind of America too. My
> beliefs? Full employment, equal economic opportunity for
> every American, a decent education for every American,
> basic health care for every working family in this country
> and a decent retirement.

The aims we used above are Dukakis'. We just shifted the focus on to the areas Dukakis wanted people to concentrate on, and avoided language that could intentionally or unintentionally be misunderstood. Indeed, Dukakis himself advises future candi-

---

*A 'liberal' means something different in every country. In American politics, a liberal is something akin to a 'radical' or a 'left-winger'.

dates to 'spend less time debating the word and more time going after the important issues'.[6] In other words, he made a mistake, and it would have been better to minimise the risk of such selective quotation.

Former British Prime Minister Margaret Thatcher made the same mistake. In a discussion on crime and responsibility she complained that people were always blaming 'society':

> . . . but there is no such thing as society, there are individual men and women, and there are families. And no government can do anything except through people, and people must look after themselves first.[7]

That is not the quote which people remember, however. What they remember is just that she said that 'there is no such thing as society'. Isolated from the context in which she initially said it, the phrase doesn't just sound libertarian, it sounds sociopathic. If you ever hear a speech criticising Margaret Thatcher's period in office, there is a nine in ten chance that you will hear that quote, and zero chance that it will be put in the context in which it was made. As she says herself, 'The most famous remark I ever made is also the most misunderstood.'[8] Below is an idea of how she could have phrased things in order to focus on what she wanted people to think about:

> People like to blame society when they break the law. But society is, after all, made up of individual men and women, and of families. And no government can do anything except through people, and people must look after themselves first.

As can be seen from the above examples, even top public speakers can get caught out by selective quotation. However, some speakers positively encourage it. They might headline their speech with an apparently shocking statement that they then go on to qualify and explain. But if you can't control the people who will report your speech to the general public, then 'shock' statements are likely to do more harm than good – especially if your target audience is at home reading about your speech in newspapers, rather than crammed into the venue and listening live.

The best advice is to think critically about your speech. Think of the worst possible way that someone could construe your words, and amend your speech accordingly. Be particularly careful if your image conforms to a stereotype. If you're known as a harsh businessperson, beware of the fact that anything you say about the need for efficiency will be taken as proof that you have no compassion for your workers. If thought of as a political manoeuvrer, beware of the fact that anything you say that sounds too smooth will be taken as proof that you're untrustworthy. In short, don't make it easy for opponents or hostile news editors to criticise and ridicule you. Try to ensure that every part of your speech can 'stand alone', and revise phrases which could easily be misinterpreted or misrepresented. Don't become famous for saying something that you never meant to say.

CHANNEL THE MEDIA'S ATTENTION

A second way to stop the media distorting the content of your speech is to structure your speech so that the segment most likely to be broadcast is the one that contains your key message. In other words, if only thirty seconds of your speech is going to be broadcast, make sure it's the *best* thirty seconds.

PLO chairman Yasser Arafat's speeches often employ a mixture of Arabic and English. Those parts of his speech which he wants the US media to emphasise – opposition to terrorism and commitment to good relations with Israel – he tends to say in English. Those parts he wishes Arab media to broadcast – his determination to secure the release of prisoners and a capital in East Jerusalem – he tends to say in Arabic. Since viewers prefer to hear people speak in their own language, and TV companies prefer not to have to translate, speeches in which he uses both languages usually result in an English section being broadcast in the US and an Arabic section being broadcast by Arab media. Arafat leads, the international media choose to follow.*

While such an approach is not available to most speakers, there are still ways to get your favourite section broadcast. With the most friendly (or most lazy) media, simply telling them which part you believe is the most important section may ensure that part is broadcast. With more critical media, one effective way of getting them to focus on the part you want them to is to tell them all of the rest of the speech in advance. That way, only the part you want them to focus on will be 'news'. This was exactly the approach used by British Labour Party leader Tony Blair in his 1994 Party conference speech. Journalists were given copies of the entire speech before it was made – except for the section on changing the Labour Party's 'socialist' constitution, the section of the speech Blair wanted the media to focus on. It worked perfectly. Media reports following the speech focussed almost exclusively on Blair's proposed constitutional change which was, a few months later, secured.

From the 'easy life' perspective of some editors, the simplest part to select is the summary at the end of your speech – yet another reason to make sure your ending is snappy, clear and forceful. Soundbites – short, clear explanations of your approach that can be understood from a thirty-second cut – are also parts of your speech that are likely to be broadcast. Soundbites do not need to be poetic or rhetorically flash (as we discussed on page 84), they just need to convey your core message in a short clip. They are often the only parts of speeches that many people ever hear, and allow speakers to engage with the undecided and uninterested who would never

---

*It is important to note that Arafat is not giving out contradictory messages: he is just offering different emphases. 'Accentuate the positive', as the old song goes.

dream of tuning in to America's *C-Span* or Britain's *Party Conference Live*. They are also very effective ways of explaining your case.

The ideal situation is one in which you are able to get your message across uncut and unedited. In reality, the only way to secure this is to insist on live transmission. This is perceived by viewers to be more risky and exciting, because there is always the possibility that something may go wrong. In fact, however, it is much safer. If you make a mistake in a *recorded* interview, it is possible that it will be the only part shown. If you do the same in a *live* broadcast, you can at least explain what you meant to say and spend the rest of the time more effectively. Live broadcasts are not a threat but an enormous opportunity. Strive for them when possible.

DON'T BE BATTERED BY INTERVIEWERS
In more deferential days, public figures got a gentle ride from television interviewers. (Interviewers, in turn, got a gentle ride from 'ordinary people', who were treated as yet another step further down the media food chain.) Nowadays, the situation is more healthy. Interviewers are more than ready to 'speak on behalf of the nation' and give hostile, testing interviews to all levels of public figures and are ready to accuse all of them of the now-clichéd cry that they 'haven't answered the question'. In return, public figures are more than ready to accuse the interviewer of conspiracy and of distorting the truth. In other words, people who have to justify themselves to the media – be it a businessperson in the local newspaper, or a President on national TV – need to be ready to stick up for themselves effectively.

For TV interviews, a key consideration is how much time you will get to present your case. Any estimate given by the programme's producers is likely to be an upper limit, so you need to think of the most concise way to put across your point. You need also to be confident – don't be cut short by an interviewer or by other speakers and (if you can do so honourably) try to ensure that you get the last word on a discussion panel.

Be careful about the pace that you speak at. Even the calmest interviewers have a buzzing mind during broadcasts – they have to watch what they say, listen to you, cue the next question, allow others to contribute and have an overriding sense of time pressure partly due to the person sitting in the control room and giving instructions through their ear-piece. This means that interviewers have a *natural tendency* to hurry up the interviewee. This often fazes first-time interviewees who have rehearsed their answers in the calm of their living room the night before. It especially fazes interviewees who have put dramatic pauses in their speeches – for a slight pause invites the interviewer to jump in and move the discussion along.

As should be clear from the preceding advice and examples, speaking through the media involves a trade-off between getting your message across to large numbers and accepting that you cannot control how that message is put out. Some interviewers try to help speakers to get their message across. Most don't. You need to decide what your minimum message is, and make sure you've said it by the end of the interview. That often means coming in with it right away. For a radio interview, you can even have your main points written down in front of you (after all, no one can see) but for TV you will have to store them in your head. A good tip is to prepare a few examples. They make your message more interesting. They also make sure that you are the expert, as they are much more likely to be accepted than statistics. For example, the doctor who relates the story of a patient who had to wait two years for treatment is usually on safer ground than the one who claims that overall health spending has been cut.

Lastly, if the interview is to be cut and especially if there are several 'takes' in filming, bear in mind that the *interviewer* will always be shown in the best light possible – so you have to stay alert through all takes and throughout all parts of the interview.

3. SUMMARY

- **All media are not the same.** Pick the media that attract your target audience.

- **TV means close-up.** It's not vain to care about your TV appearance – presentation is part of winning people over. Make sure the background, too, reinforces your message.

- **TV images are normally seen in the home.** As Neil Kinnock discovered, TV audiences want something different from the crowd at the venue.

- **Media means editing; editing means distortion.** Make sure your comments can 'stand alone'. Remember what happened to Dukakis and Thatcher, and don't become famous for saying something you never meant to say.

- **Channel the media's attention.** Get them to focus on the key parts of your speech. Or go live – so that your message will be heard in the context *you* set.

- **Don't be battered by interviewers.** Make sure you get a fair hearing, and be prepared to be politely firm.

SPEAKING IN BUSINESS AND COMMITTEE MEETINGS

1. BACKGROUND

Some business events – such as large meetings of shareholders – involve exactly the same public speaking skills as have previously been discussed. Board meetings or committee-style meetings, however, require very different skills: they need the speaker to be more conversational and more personal, and they therefore merit special consideration. However, so that this section is as wide ranging as possible, we will discuss all forms of 'around the table discussions' – be they meetings at work, meetings of a local charity or even an informal family discussion over the dinner table. Head of a multinational, secretary of your regional Amnesty International group or aggrieved teenager – this section will show you how to put your case.

A well-run meeting is, of course, about more than public speaking. For example, a good chairperson will provide a strong agenda for the meeting that allows everyone a chance to contribute and the participants will have discussed key matters with each other before the meeting. Most importantly, efficient committee meetings and negotiation processes require good time management, clear goals and hard work. Such strategic aims are, however, not the concern of this chapter. Here we will consider the more subtle art of putting your case – how to apply the advice contained in this book to making powerful arguments in meetings.

You are strongly advised to read the earlier sections of this book before delving into this chapter but we recap the most relevant points below. These are the 'ground rules' for making a successful speech in a business meeting.

1. *Know your stuff.* On pages 27 to 28, we saw the importance of knowing your topic well. Check, therefore, that your own objectives for the meeting are SMART (specific, measurable, achievable, realistic and well-timed).[1] You should also have a feeling for the reasons people may have for objecting to your demands or proposals. Moreover, you should have a feeling for the underlying principles behind other people's positions. For example, if someone in a board meeting proposes a merger, are they really interested in the merger itself, or are they enticed by the extra personal benefits? It is important to know how the other participants in the meeting think, so that you can understand (or see through) their comments.

2. *Not just words.* On pages 125 to 127, we examined how getting people actively to participate in something can change their behaviour as well as their minds. Thus, after winning over your fellow committee members during the meeting, it is often a good idea to follow up the point with a memo or an e-mail. Convert persuasion to action.

3. *Persuasive arguments are intellectually rigorous.* Either in negotiations or as part of a committee, your viewpoint will often be challenged and opposed. It is therefore very important to ensure that the arguments you advance are solid. Pages 60 to 87 dealt with some key ways to check that your arguments are not easily rebuffed. In particular, we analysed how to use insight and evidence in a speech, and saw how contradictions, truisms and misinformation can leave a speech open to attack. These pages deserve re-reading, as they will improve your ability to spot a weak argument.

4. *Find your colleagues' argumentative baseline.* As explained on pages 54 to 58, every argument that is advanced is based on some assertions or assumptions. A persuasive argument is

thus rooted in assertions that are acceptable to the people listening. For example, we considered President Reagan's famous 'Evil Empire' speech, which he delivered to a Christian convention in 1983. Much of its success derived from the fact that Reagan described his topic (the Cold War) in terms of a battle for religious morality; he tuned his topic to suit his Christian audience. Similarly, you must be fully aware of other participants' aims and viewpoints. They are most easily persuaded when your arguments are based on things that they believe in and advance causes they care about.

5. *Language is crucial to persuasion.* Pages 89 to 109 outlined the importance of language when framing arguments. We shall see below that the words used to frame questions can help cue the answer. In addition, the words you use can create rapport with other negotiators or fellow committee members. Why do some people prefer to say 'I can *see* that concept', whereas others may say 'I can *grasp* what you're saying'?[2] The words we use reflect our view of the world. If you can tune your phrases and arguments to match those of other committee members, then a subtle form of rapport can be built.

6. *Style and presentation are always important.* A good level of volume and eye contact are the best ways to engage an audience and make them attentive. On pages 15 to 24, however, we saw that good style is about more than just speaking clearly. In committee meetings, it is particularly important not to appear closed to the suggestions of others. Your style therefore needs to be polite ('that's a fair point, but . . .' rather than 'no') and you need to look attentive – even if you have understood the kernel of someone's argument and are busy thinking of a reply. It is also worth re-reading pages 119 to 124, which describe how the time of day and the venue can both affect how people respond to each other's speeches.

7. *Be prepared for audio-visual work.* As we discussed on pages 133 to 142, audio-visuals can significantly enhance the power of your arguments. Their successful use, however, depends on good preparation. In particular, you should check what equipment is available at the venue, and have a back-up plan in case it fails. Moreover, each audio-visual aid has its own strengths and weaknesses and the pages referenced above will help you to decide which piece of equipment to use.

8. *Show respect for others.* You need to allow others to contribute in the meeting. The ideal committee member is keen and silently attentive during the speeches of others. Your expression while you listen to others speak is very important, for it is easy to disrupt a speaker by assuming a puzzled look (or, in the extreme, laughing at them) during their speech or to encourage another by nodding in agreement. The worst committee meetings are full of *ad hominem* comments. Personal insults are unlikely to draw sympathy from the rest of the committee.

The eight points listed above are a focussed summary of the main sections of this book, and apply whether speaking to a large audience or to a committee of three. In this chapter, however, we will concentrate on issues that are particularly important when speaking 'around a table', such as:

- How to frame questions
- How to negotiate
- How to win from the chair.

2. HOW TO FRAME QUESTIONS
Round table discussions necessarily involve more questions and interjections than do speeches to large audiences. The key is to make sure that your questions are effective.

THE DIRECTED QUESTION

In some languages, questions are not answered with a simple 'yes' or 'no'. For instance, if you ask someone in Welsh, 'Am I late?', they will reply 'You are', or if you ask, 'Is your sister coming?', they will reply 'She is'. Unfortunately, the English speaker simply replies to such questions with the words 'yes' or 'no', and this can cloud people's insight into the subtleties of questioning.

The questions you pose will tend to have a *natural answer*, and a successful speaker realises that a question should therefore be phrased in a way that cues the most profitable natural answer and natural *style* of answer. Suppose, for example, that you sit on a road traffic committee. You are proposing the installation of speed bumps, but other members prefer speed cameras. Below are some of the questions you might ask in discussion. Examine the natural answer (and the style of that answer) that might come back at you.

1. 'What's the problem with speed bumps?'
   The natural answer to this begins 'It's . . .'. The question cues other speakers to list all the problems with speed bumps (of which there are many). They are not pushed to think about their possible benefits, and are free to rail against your proposal.
2. 'Would there be at least an opportunity to try speed bumps in some areas?'
   The natural answer to this very reasonable question is a very reasonable response. At the very worst, the natural answer would begin 'Well, yes, there may be some opportunities, but . . .'. However, even in this case, critics have been forced to concede some ground. They are pressed to admit some value in your idea. They cannot give an unreasonable answer to a reasonable question.

It would be wrong to conclude that the second method of asking questions is *always* better. The aim is simply to prompt the natural answer that is most suitable for your purposes. For example, watch good lawyers in court and you will see how they alter the style of their questions. If cross-examining a witness, the lawyer might appear very reasonable in order for them to respond reasonably – and thus yield ground. So she might, for example, say 'Do you think there's a possibility that, in the heat of the moment, a harmless tussle may have looked more violent than it actually was?' Sometimes, however, the lawyer may need to press the witness a bit more: 'The fact is that you don't like foreign people, do you?' In each case, the style of the question depends on the circumstances.

The easiest way to see the natural answer to a question is to replace all the substantive words (like 'speed bumps' in the example earlier) with nonsensical words. Then ask yourself the question again and note how you begin your reply. Gaining a feeling for how people are likely to respond to questions makes you a sharper, more switched-on and more persuasive speaker.

There is an interesting corollary to the concept of the natural answer. The words used to ask the question cue the speaker to respond in a certain way, so in the examples above, 'What's the problem with . . .' cued the opponent to respond combatively with a list of problems. The *type* of response is thus cued almost as soon as the question is asked. However, the *arguments* for the response require more thought. Hence, if you are asked a question that is so short that you do not have time to think, you may well have cued the style of your response (for example, an aggressive one: 'What's the problem? I'll tell him what the problem is all right . . .') but not had time to think of any substantive points. The danger then is that you may be left stumbling for words and give a weak reply. The way to avoid this is by staying alert, being on top of your brief and not feeling pressured to respond straightaway.

For example, in a recent BBC radio interview, a spokesperson for a teachers' union was criticising proposals that he felt would lead to further selection in education. A quick question by the interviewer caught him off-guard:

Interviewer: But couldn't we be doing more for our most gifted pupils?

Spokesperson: No.

If the spokesperson had thought a bit longer, he could have replied something like 'Yes, we could and should be doing more for *all* our pupils, and here's how . . .' but the style of question had surprised him. In seeking to avoid giving in, he ended up looking unhelpful.

THE LOYAL QUESTION

Many people in hierarchical situations may be reluctant to ask critical questions, fearing that their future prospects might suffer. The result instead may be that the whole organisation suffers from carrying on with an approach that should have never been followed. So how can you ask a critical question without appearing disloyal? One way is to ask it as someone else's question. Imagine you are a member of a board organising a takeover. You feel it is a waste of money but are worried that, in saying so, you might lose your job. Instead of asking 'isn't this a waste of money?' or saying nothing, you could instead comment:

> I can see the arguments for the deal, I'm just wondering what we can say to shareholders who might complain that it's too expensive.

The issue has been raised without you being seen as an obstacle. By using the word 'we' and framing the criticism in terms of an 'other', you have conveyed the unity of purpose of the group and, at the same time, have been able to raise doubts about the policy. Moreover, if you can find *something* that you genuinely like about the policy, then say so explicitly – as it makes your support sound more genuine – before you follow up with '. . . but how can you help me to sell this to my party?' or '. . . if there was a Doubting Thomas, how would you convince him?'

and '. . . but how can we overcome the problems we encountered with this last year?' Don't sound like a person who causes problems, sound like someone who foresees them.

3. HOW TO NEGOTIATE

Another key feature of 'round table' discussions and business meetings is that your arguments need to be directed to specific individuals, rather than to a collective audience. This requires you to think carefully about the person you are addressing.

KNOW WHO YOU'RE TALKING TO

You cannot persuade everybody in the same way. You therefore need to understand the person you are talking to and to frame your arguments in a way that appeals to them. It would obviously be impossible to provide a complete description of how best to persuade every type of person who may or may not sit on your committee. Instead, we will describe four different methods for framing arguments in front of a committee and then examine what *type* of person would respond best to each method. Real people, however, do not fit into neat stereotypes. You should therefore treat the stereotypical characters below as a *game* to sharpen your abilities in tailoring arguments to fit the committee members, rather than a formula for persuading people.

1. Sometimes it is best to frame your arguments like a *consultation*, rather than as a briefing or a lecture. In other words, you *involve* the other person in the argument, and therefore implicitly show that you value their comments. You might frame your arguments as a question: 'I was thinking about this as a proposal, but how do you think it could be improved?' You may even *deliberately* leave part of your argument in need of clarification, in order to give the other person an opportunity to respond or to restate it better themselves.

This method of framing arguments is often good for persuading older, more senior and respected people. Perhaps a project manager, a committee chairperson, or (for kitchen table discussions) a parent. When the arguments are framed in a consultative manner, you demonstrate your respect for their knowledge and experience. If you don't show such respect, it invites them to find something to criticise in your argument – if only to prove that their powers have not faded.

For example, one of the authors once had a project manager who hated having things clearly explained to him. He would become restless and feel insulted if briefed in too obvious a manner. The answer was then to explain things less completely in conversation, or to provide briefings that led him to the right conclusion without explicitly stating what that conclusion was. The project manager could then feel that he had come to his own decisions, and that the briefing was merely a spark for his *own* thoughts. And in case you yourself are such a person, we'll add no more explanation on this.

2. Sometimes it is best to press your case gently. You might, for instance, qualify your arguments with statements like 'Sorry if this is a bit naïve, but . . .' or 'This is obviously not my field, but . . .' or 'Correct me if I'm wrong . . .' The style you adopt is not brash, but gentle.

This method of framing arguments often works best on 'nice guy' stereotypes. A gentle and highly ethical person will generally not be happy about demolishing such an easy target. This method of framing arguments therefore encourages sympathetic people to side with you, especially if your arguments are met with forceful opposition from another committee member.

Consider a defendant who represents themselves in court, rather than employing a lawyer. Many juries are very sympathetic in such a case, as they don't like to see an uneven battle between a canny prosecution lawyer and a humble, unskilled defendant. Good prosecution lawyers therefore press their arguments very gently in these circumstances.

This approach also prevents you from losing face if you do turn out to be wrong. It is therefore a safer approach than brashness if you are not yet sure of your point. However, if the answers you get are less than impressive, you can change tack and move to the next type of approach.

3. Sometimes it is best to appear confident in your own knowledge of the situation. You might phrase questions as direct statements – 'Obviously, you've checked these figures for . . .' – and directly rebut points that other committee members raise. You might even deliberately avoid style and panache in your presentation – so as to appear like someone obsessed with the matter at hand, rather than its presentation. Technocrats – central bankers, chief medical officers, military officials and others – often play up to this stereotype to make themselves seem apolitical and 'scientific' in their analysis. They are usually more trusted than politicians and journalists, partly for this reason.

This method of framing arguments works best when locked in debate with a self-confident shark – such as an eager, ambitious, younger employee who prides himself on his ability to get his own way. This kind of stereotype needs to be handled in almost exactly the opposite way as the 'nice guy'. He will have no qualms about seeing a naïve committee member lose a debate and will equate 'naïve' with 'pushover'. However, people who possess this type of character trait are often too self-protective to enter into confrontational debate with someone who appears to have expertise. You can therefore win a debate with such a person by scaring them away. When you frame your arguments like an expert, you appear too knowledgeable to be manipulated and you signal to them that they won't come out of the battle unscathed.

4. Sometimes it is best to say little. State your position concisely and without repetition. Then stay silent and still. Wait. Allow the other person to fill up the room with sounds. Do not rush to respond after they have spoken, but maintain your silence.

This method of framing arguments can be very powerful indeed when you are speaking to someone more junior than yourself. Perhaps you are the boss talking to an employee, or the chairperson addressing a new committee member. You need to be in a position to *control* the silence, so if you might appear disrespectful by remaining silent, or if other people might butt in, then this technique will not work. But why *does* this technique work? After your opponent has finished speaking, the silence is a cue for you to speak. If, however, you maintain the silence and don't rush to respond, you will often find that your opponent waffles to fill up the embarrassing silence. The silence prompts them to say *more* than they intended, and this puts them at a disadvantage. A well-held silence can often prompt the opponent to admit to weaknesses in their own argument and then respond to them – in effect, continuing the argument on your behalf.

This same principle can apply to haggling. If you, the customer, are reluctant to talk, then exuberant traders will often fill the awkward silence by haggling against themselves on your behalf: 'OK, you obviously think it's not worth 200 dollars, how about 100?' Silence can be a great weapon for forcing people to say more than they want to.

In summary, you can only frame your arguments persuasively if you know what sort of person you are addressing. When speaking to a large group, such targeting is necessarily very general. When speaking to individuals, however, you can and should *tailor your arguments to the person that you are addressing*. The stereotypes listed above are obviously too one-dimensional to be real people, but thinking about different character traits is a good way to gain insight into how to tune your arguments to fit the person. Many people do this very well naturally in conversation and day-to-day life, but forget it when called upon to speak in public. That is why we have included it in this book.

SUBTLE RAPPORT

In the earlier sections of the book, we discussed how the presentation of your arguments can affect the audience's response (see pages 119–132). In a committee meeting, you are observed much more closely – so your style, body language and movements are even more important for building rapport.

Rapport is built in a number of ways. Remembering facts about another person (such as the names of their children) and taking an interest in their life are normal everyday ways that people show they want to 'get on' with others. In many countries, showing an interest in your opposite number's life is also a necessary precondition for striking a business deal.

Note that we said 'taking an interest' in the person's life. Many books have been written describing subtle ways to charm and compliment people. They've normally got big bold letters on the front cover, are printed on cheap paper and use jargon phrases like 'interact with the heart channel'. These books should all be treated with caution. Fluent linguists aren't made by awkwardly stammering out words at locals from a phrase-book – they are made when people immerse themselves in a language. The same is true for learning how to become the kind of person who people can 'get on with'. There really is no point learning insincere formulae for how to compliment and charm people. In fact, compliments can sometimes be very patronising (just imagine going up to Albert Einstein and complimenting him on his physics), because in complimenting people, you often have to control the conversation, and if you do this confidently, it may irritate your employer, your new girlfriend/boyfriend's parents, or indeed anyone else who thinks that *they* should be in control. Charm learnt from a book normally ruins people's ability to be sensitive to such questions of respect. A better approach is to become genuinely interested in the other person's point of view – even if it means mentally forcing yourself to listen to and think about their point of view.

With those caveats in mind, there are a number of ways in which you can make your points more palatable to people. Verbal techniques for helping to create rapport abound, the most common of which is *voice matching*, which is a tool used widely by telephone salespeople.[3] In its simplest form, voice matching involves altering the tone, speed, rhythm and pitch of your voice so as to match that of the person you are talking to (but without sounding like you are mimicking them). The reason that telesales staff learn 'voice matching' is that it is a subtle way of building rapport with the customer. There are underlying reasons that cause people to speak loudly, or in high-pitched tones or at great pace. So if you match somebody's voice, it suggests that you feel the same underlying reasons that they do. Common phrases like 'she's my kind of person' or 'we just naturally think like each other' reflect the fact that we befriend people of similar outlook and values to ourselves. We like people like us.

How can we apply this to a committee discussion? Obviously, you can use voice matching to try to gain rapport with a committee member who you are attempting to persuade. It can contribute an extra appeal to your arguments, or at least ensure that your voice is not unnecessarily irritating to them. It is also a useful way of calming people down – particularly if you are the committee chairperson or another senior figure. If someone is shouting angrily, then they will often hate being talked to in a calm, soft, slow voice. 'Calming voices' can often sound patronising. The contrast between an angry voice of one committee member and a mediator's calm voice is an obvious signal that says, 'I think you're being unreasonable'. Much better then, to approximately match the voice of the angry person, but apply just a little less anger. This signals that you understand their anger, but lowers the heat of the discussion.

This is not the only subtle method for building rapport. One of many other techniques is 'word matching' – which works in an analogous way to voice matching. Generally, however, the most effective way of building rapport is to frame your proposals in terms that interest the listeners. This point is discussed extensively in earlier sections of the book, so see pages 53 to 58 if you need a recap.

4. HOW TO WIN FROM THE CHAIR

As stated earlier, great speakers don't just ask themselves what they are going to say, they ask themselves how they are going to be. The same is true with great chairpersons or team leaders. In this section, we will describe the sort of style of chairing that you should aim for. Part of being a good chairperson lies in realising that style alone is not sufficient, so the advice here is powerful, but incomplete.

The first thing to aim for is fairness. Once you are fair, then you need to be *seen to be fair*. Unless you are specifically rebuking or praising someone, then your tone, manner, eye contact and body language should be the same when addressing every member of the committee. While it is easy to maintain this in calm meetings, prejudices can easily show through when you interject to stop heckling, or caution members not to interrupt others' speeches.

The second matter to aim for is consent. The chairperson needs to carry the will of the committee. Your gestures need to reflect this – look at the committee when speaking, rather than focussing on your notes or on the most attractive committee member. Watch your language for non-consensual phrases like 'I'll tell you what we should do . . .' or 'The best thing is . . .' Try more inclusive phraseology such as 'Would people agree if . . .' or 'I'd be interested if people had any objections, but shall we try . . .' or 'Am I right in thinking . . .' Consent is also important when putting matters to a vote – try to provide the committee with various options, so that they can feel they have a hand in decision-making. Former British Prime Minister John Major gives some sound advice on consensual chairmanship: '[Let your] own views be known in private, see potential dissenters ahead of the meeting, encourage discussion, and sum up after it.'[4]

The next virtue of a good chairperson is control. Much of this is strategic, such as planning an agenda or good time management skills. However, control also means alertness. Is someone being continuously and unfairly interrupted by other committee members? Then call for order. Is someone waffling endlessly and not making a point? Then stop them and try to phrase what they are saying more concisely yourself. Is someone obstructing business for tactical reasons? Then reason with them inside or outside the meeting. Has some issue been left half-discussed? Then bring the issue out into the open, rather than leaving it festering at the back of people's minds. Feeling confident in your position and staying alert are the foundations of control.

Set the tone. The chairperson's mood affects the whole meeting. If discussions are getting unnecessarily heated, then use voice matching to calm the atmosphere. Or halt the bickering members and ask for someone else's opinion. If the purpose of the meeting is to brainstorm, then pitch in with some suggestions as well – but don't put people off 'free thinking' by being dominant. If the purpose of the meeting is to keep people in touch with each other's work, then ensure that you already know what people have been working on. If the meeting has to be efficient, then keep your welcoming comments and your own interjections short and businesslike. Your behaviour should reflect the way you want the meeting to run.

Be an architect of compromise. As an ostensibly impartial figure, the chairperson is also the peace broker. You can help the committee to reach decisions quickly by finding ground that both sides in a dispute can concede. A good peace broker will find benefits for both parties to take away from negotiations. Following the 1998 Good Friday Agreement on the future of

Northern Ireland, Irish Nationalists and Republicans claimed triumph because they had secured the foundation of new North–South Irish political bodies, the release of political prisoners and representation within the government of Northern Ireland. Similarly, Ulster Unionists claimed triumph because they had secured the right of self-determination, a new devolved government and a removal of the Republic of Ireland's constitutional claim on the North. Both sides could not, of course, simultaneously defeat the other, but good negotiators had found many different triumphs for each side to sell to its own supporters. Importantly, the triumphs on both sides were significant – not just patronising gestures. The triumphs also arose from creating new structures (such as the new North–South political bodies and the new Northern Irish assembly), and this is a good example to any would-be peace broker: daring to innovate and suggesting new projects *outside* the current dispute are good ways to achieve compromise.

In helping to achieve compromise, it is often helpful to disentangle the issues involved in the dispute. Too many disputes are caused by one side refusing to apologise or yield until the other side concedes over an entirely different point. 'Why should I apologise to him for hitting him? He wrecked my bike' is the standard sort of argument that parents have to resolve. Such 'them and us' situations are dangerous. As a chairperson (or parental peace broker), you should *atomise* the dispute, considering each issue separately and in parallel, rather than deciding who is right and who is wrong overall. Therefore, you need to break the dispute over the bike into its constituent parts: 1. Who hit who? and 2. Who wrecked the bike? Once both parties can acknowledge their separate mistakes, then act on that – perhaps by getting them to apologise simultaneously – but don't let a sense of *overall* blame hang over the negotiations, even in simple disputes about bikes.

The chairperson's *style* is also central to settling disputes and achieving compromise. Where possible, try to credit and acknowledge the suggestions of the aggrieved parties. For example, you might say, 'When drawing up the strategy for next year, I suggest we take John's suggestion that . . .' especially if John was one of the combatants in the discussion over that strategy. Acknowledgement from the chairperson can often work wonders. Phrases such as 'I can see you're angry about this' or 'You've obviously put a lot of work into this' are very important for signalling to the committee members that their complaints have been noted and that their statements have been considered. There is then less incentive for them to overact or overstate their position from then on in order to gain recognition.

The final characteristic you will need is that of a good manager. Be aware of your committee members' work. Actively seek out examples of tasks that they have completed successfully so you can praise them; be aware of their ability to work without help; avoid divisive comparisons between committee members and set a good example. Talk and convince yourself into being a sharp, active, approachable manager. Strive to avoid the complaint commonly levied at committees – that they take minutes and last hours.

5. SUMMARY

- **Don't ignore the rest of this book.** There are eight topics in the main section of the book that deserve revision if you want to improve your ability to speak in committee meetings. Look back at pages 159 to 162 if you want to remind yourself what they are.

- **Frame questions carefully**. A well-cued and snappy question can leave your opponent stumbling. The 'loyal question' technique can be used to raise your concerns to a single-minded boss. In both cases, however, you should frame your question so as to prompt the right sort of natural answer.

- **Know who you're talking to.** The way you frame your arguments should depend on the person you're talking to. Look back at the four different styles of argument that we considered on pages 166 to 170.

- **Rapport can be built in subtle ways.** Voice matching and word matching can contribute to creating a good rapport with others. If done badly, however, they can look like mimicry. The best routes for rapport are to be genuinely interested in the other person's point of view, and to frame your proposals in terms that they find interesting.

- **The style of the chairperson influences the whole meeting.** Aim to be fair, consensual, in control, a tone-setter, a peace broker and a manager in your words and in your gestures. Talk yourself into adopting these characteristics and imagine yourself as a good chair. Then go forth and do.

SPEAKING AT WEDDINGS

> ### Relevant Sections in the Rest of This Book
>
> This chapter should not be read in isolation from the rest of the book. The following sections are particularly important for speeches at weddings:
>

1. DON'T WORRY: THIS IS THE EASIEST SPEECH YOU'LL EVER MAKE

Giving a speech at a wedding is, for many people, the first time they've spoken in public since they donned their nativity costume and asked in a loud voice if there was any room at the Inn. Fear and nerves are often unnecessarily great. For instance, if you could look into the best man's mind on the wedding day, what do you think he would be thinking about? How to ensure the couple has a good day? How to make sure everything runs smoothly? Perhaps, but for many best men, there is one thought that hangs over others: the speech. In fact, however, wedding speeches are the easiest speeches you will ever make. Why?

The first reason why wedding speeches are far easier than you might fear is that the audience is willing you to succeed. You just don't get hostile audiences at weddings. They all are generous with applause, in good spirits and, most importantly, drunk. They will laugh more graciously and listen more attentively than any other audience you will encounter. They do not expect to be convinced or 'won over' by an argument, they do not seek to be educated or taught – they simply want to listen to stories about the bride and groom and are determined to have a good time.

The second reason is that the content of your speech is your expert topic. Weddings and wedding speeches are celebrations of the bride, groom and their families. Those speaking at the wedding are best placed to talk about these people, and in that sense, the speakers at a wedding are world experts in their subject. Nobody else on the planet could do a better job.

But it's even better than that. You have a whole host of material to back up your own stories, as quotations and jokes abound on the subject of love and marriage. There are few topics more universal or more widely written about. There is a whole genre of jokes and banter, too, that are based entirely on the formalities of the wedding day itself. Many bridegrooms' speeches, for example, contain throwaway lines such as; 'Now *my* job here today is just to thank people, but I'm told that my best man has to be absolutely blindingly funny.'

Best of all, you only need to fill five minutes' worth of speech. Selecting the very best bits from all this material in order to fill only a few minutes is a speechwriter's dream.

All these reasons are solid facts with which to kill worry. Material for your speech is vast, and the audience will be willing you to succeed. The conditions for speaking are ideal, and, unless you deliberately set out to offend or disgust the audience, your speech cannot ruin the day. People have come to watch a couple get married and one speech, however bad it is, will not ruin this. After the alcohol wears off, the audience won't even remember it.

2. THE FORMAT OF THE SPEECHES

Unfortunately, even the most inventive and radical people can turn into compulsive rule-followers when faced with wedding etiquette. Don't let the customs faze you; many of them are suited to a bygone era where cross-cultural marriages, divorced parents and multiple best men were rare. Don't follow these customs for the sake of 'tradition'; the ultimate judges of the format of the speeches should be the families involved in the wedding.

For a 'traditional' English wedding, the speeches normally follow the pattern shown in the table below. It is not immutable, and it is common practice at Jewish weddings (and others) for the groom to speak after the best man. Another, more modern, tradition is for the head bridesmaid to offer a toast of thanks or to speak alongside the best man. At some larger weddings, moreover, the family may want a distinguished guest to say a few words. (In this case, it is usual for the guest to follow the best man's speech. The groom or best man may then offer a toast of thanks following the guest's speech.) All such variations are, again, at the discretion of the families of the bride and groom.

Speech number	Speaker	Main thrust of speech	Typical toast at end of speech
1	Bride's father (or person who gave her away)	Welcomes everyone – because he's paying and therefore he's the host. Talks about the bride and her childhood. Also talks about getting to know the groom and welcomes him into the family.	'To the health and happiness of the bride and groom'
2	Groom	Main purpose is to thank people. He thanks the bride's family and compliments the bride. May talk for a bit about his bride.	'The bridesmaids' *or*, if the bride is speaking: 'The bride'

		Thanks his parents and may tell some stories about his upbringing. Thanks the assistants (best man, bridesmaids, ushers, helpers and so on) and may include a story or two about the best man.	
3 (Not universal but increasingly popular.)	Bride	The bride's and the groom's speeches are similar in form. She may want to thank both sets of parents and also her bridesmaids. She might also want to tell a few stories about the groom.	'The bridesmaids'
4	Best man	Formally replies on behalf of the bridesmaids. The best man provides a younger view of the couple. As the bride's father talks extensively about the bride, the best man's speech focusses mainly on the groom. He may also talk about the couple. Ends with the programme for the rest of the evening. Additional duties may include reading telegrams and acting as a compère for further events	'The bride and groom' *and* 'The host and hostess'

We have tried to condense the etiquette into the essentials listed in the table above. Some outdated customs still linger, however. Most notable of these is the expectation that the best man will read telegrams from absent guests. (The idea being that if you can't be bothered to turn up to the wedding, everyone who has made the effort to attend is forced to listen to your greetings.) A sensible best man will realise that this is a singularly lame way to end his speech, and will either display the telegrams on a board and invite the audience to look at them afterwards, or invent several humorous telegrams as a means of injecting humour into the speech.

Another tradition that is common in some parts of America, Ireland and other countries is an 'open-mike' session at the end of the speeches, where anyone can add their best wishes. This is, sadly, seldom enjoyable. In most cases, the audience feel that the open-mike session is less worthy of their attention, and it just prolongs the agony of sitting in a hot room, next to people you don't know and needing the bathroom. If the families of the bride and groom decide that they do want an open-mike session, then it is essential that someone (usually the best man) strictly regulates the length and number of speakers by acting as a compère.

3. THE DO-IT-YOURSELF UNIQUE SPEECH KIT

We don't believe in prescribing set or sample speeches for a wedding. The artificial sample speeches that you find in many books cannot provide the speaker with any more than a mediocre and lacklustre speech. This is because such sample speeches neglect the one element that is essential – stories and tales about your particular bride and groom. Sample speeches typically run something like this:

> I was there when Oscar and Jane first met. Oscar and I had gone to watch the football together. Jane was sitting behind and spilled her drink all over us! I don't think Oscar minded, though – he was just working out how to steal a kiss from Jane!!

Such a scenario is too specific to be of any use to anyone. Also, it illustrates two common failures of sample speeches. First, the material is mind-numbingly dull and second, it ages quickly – the 'oh-aren't-I-being-saucy' references to kissing are well out of date. So put these ideas out of your mind – they are artificial, tedious and guaranteed to disappoint.

In the following pages, we shall instead spark *your own* creativity and imagination. We want you to write the speeches, not us.

HOW TO AVOID GETTING INTO TROUBLE

Before we look at the content of individual speeches, some brief advice on how to avoid causing trouble with your speech. One lacklustre speech won't ruin the wedding day – as the bride and groom, not the speeches, are the main focus of attention. However, an offensive speech will cause problems. Among the long-lost relatives and unknown friends, there are likely to be people in the audience who are more easily offended than you might think. We have compiled a list of things to watch out for:

- *Check the duties you are expected to perform.* Who are you supposed to toast and thank? If in doubt, see the table on pages 179–180 – but make sure that all the speakers know what each other's roles are.
- *Check the names and how they are pronounced.* It is surprisingly common to hear speakers at weddings mispronounce the names of the participants. Does William prefer to be called Will, and is Nicola usually a 'Nicky'? On a day when everyone wants to feel special, getting someone's name wrong is a big *faux pas*.
- *Check sensitive areas.* Enquire discreetly to see if there are any family feuds, or any close relatives who are especially sensitive about certain subjects. However sophisticated your speech is, the sight of Auntie storming out of the room in disgust will make you look crass.
- *Don't be jealous.* It is quite common to see speakers sitting on the top table and looking jealous of the applause that other speakers receive. Don't. Wishing others ill in order to make your own performance stand out is a true sign of amateurism.

It will be noticed by audience members and other speakers and will damage the atmosphere.

- *Watch how much you drink.* It's easy to pop into the pub before the wedding and have a drink to 'stiffen the nerves'. It's also easy to recline in your chair during the wedding breakfast and let the waiter top up your glass of wine or champagne. Such easy drinking often leads to problematic speaking. Like drinking and driving, alcohol may well give you superhuman confidence, but it also gives you subhuman abilities.

GENERAL TIPS FOR A GOOD WEDDING SPEECH

The points above provide a guide to avoiding *problems* with your speech. In order to compose a successful wedding speech, however, there are some further tips that are worth considering.

The first of these is to *plan well in advance*. Carry a pad with you, and leave one by your bed. Whenever you think of a suitable anecdote or observation relating to the bride or groom, note it down. As we mentioned on page 10, things will strike you at odd times – in the shower, just before you fall asleep or while watching television. If you note down the ideas, anecdotes and stories as they occur to you, then you are effectively writing your speech continuously. Compile all the jottings and scribbled ideas in an envelope and let them accumulate into a stock of material over the many weeks you will (probably) have to prepare. Don't let your mind be filled with things you wish you'd said *after* the wedding is over.

The second point is to focus – in a realistic way – on the bride and groom. Don't let jokes or stories about the wedding guests dominate your speech. The main content of all the speeches should be stories about the bride and groom. That is, of course, the whole purpose of the speeches and also what everybody wants to, expects to and is waiting to hear. Having said that, however, your speech needs to be realistic. Unyieldingly glowing and fawning tributes said with lip-quivering piety always make the speaker look ridiculous. Wedding speeches are best when the context of the speech is that the bride and groom are wonderful, but mixed with good-natured stories about their awkward mannerisms and embarrassing moments. Portrayals of purely good or evil characters are always unconvincing. (See the modern trend for film villains to have a humane side and film heroes to have a dark side.) You don't have to pretend that the bride and groom are perfect in order to say that they are perfect *for each other*.

Third, *watch your use of comedy*. A wedding speech doesn't have to be stand-up comedy – and people don't expect it to be. Instead, base your speech not on jokes, but on anecdotes about the bride and groom. (See also the section on anecdotes and comedy on pages 71 to 75.) The sort of stories you'd tell at a dinner party or when speaking on the phone to your friends are ideal. People tend to laugh very easily at such stories because they are true and because, knowing the characters involved, they find them endearing. In addition, good humour needs to connect with the audience – so whilst very few will mind innuendo, outright vulgarity might at least offend someone's granny, even if these days it is more likely to make the vicar laugh than to walk out.

Fourth, *use props*. Funny objects can work just as well as funny words. Photographs of the bride and groom, for example, can be immensely effective. Some best men distribute copies of such photographs to the audience and invite them to submit witty captions. (This not only gets the guests talking, but it provides the best man with speech material.) We ourselves once saw a great speech where the best man produced items of clothing that the groom loved to wear, but the bride was determined to throw away (favourite jumpers with holes in them and the like). Even those who hadn't seen the dubious images of the groom wearing these jumpers found it funny, as it provided a personal insight into his dress sense. Most important, however, is the fact that this sort of thing can *only* be done with props – so don't feel that your speech has to be entirely verbal.

The final tip: *keep it short*. Drunk people are easily amused but quickly bored. Sit down while the audience still wants more.

With those points in mind, we will now look at each of the main speeches individually. We will pose a series of questions. Read them slowly and let your mind wander and recall relevant tales and stories. You should acquire many more than you need to fill a five- to ten-minute speech. After using the do-it-yourself speech kit, most people find that the problem is deciding what to leave out of the speech, rather than what to put in.*

SPEECH BY THE BRIDE'S FATHER

This speech welcomes the guests, provides a commentary on the bride and usually ends by welcoming the groom into the family. Let's consider the elements of the talk:

I: The welcome

This part is straightforward. A sincere, honest welcome to the guests and a line about how good the bride and groom look is all that is required. Let the questions below trigger your thoughts to see if there is anything else that is worth including at the beginning of your speech.

- *Has anybody come from especially far to attend the wedding?* If so, you may want to acknowledge this.
- *Did anything happen during the day itself that you might want to comment on?* Topical humour goes down really well, so anything worth adding a line or two about – a cameraman who fell over, a sudden downpour of rain and so on – will usually raise a laugh.
- *Are there any stories from the planning of the wedding?* Did the groom accidentally book the wrong band to play, or did the

---

*Note that our guidance is based on a traditional English wedding, both in format and length of speeches. If you decide to alter the length of the speeches, it might be worth reading all the sections here, rather than only the one relevant to you.

couple forget to send out invitations, or was there a story about the wedding list or the suit hire? Good-natured anecdotes of this type are ideal.

II: The bride's background

The person giving the bride away normally knows her very well indeed. You no doubt have years of stories about her. Let us try to help you by directing your thoughts. Read the points below and just let your mind wander as you do so, letting anecdotes and stories return.

- *Does she have any mannerisms or character traits?* A passion for work, or shopping, or bad TV programmes? A funny smile? Was she a devoted servant to her pets when she was young? What do you find endearing about her?
- *What's her job?* Did she make any cringeworthy mistakes when she first started working there? Did she do anything at work that made you proud – such as getting promoted quickly or excelling in her field?
- *Does she have any hobbies or obsessions?* Was she into awful music as a kid? People's musical tastes change very quickly and it often raises a laugh for them to be reminded of the sort of music they liked (and clothes they wore) when they were young – particularly if their *father* is the person teasing their tastes. What activity does she do in her spare time that really defines her?
- *What are your favourite memories of her?* Was it when she received a degree or got her first job? Was it some prank she played on you when she was young?

III: Getting to know the groom

Before welcoming the groom into the family, you might tell a story or two about him.

- *What were your first impressions on meeting him?* Was he quiveringly nervous and polite? Had he made a special effort to dress up to meet you? How did your daughter describe him before you met him?

- *What do you think of him as a son-in-law?* Has he done anything noteworthy for your daughter? Has she changed in any way since first dating him? What are the qualities that you admire most in him?

IV: Ending

To conclude you may want to offer a few lines of advice to the couple. This may either be serious, a quotation, or a humorous line. It could even be all three; 'Now remember, John, as you marry our daughter, what Marcel Achard once said: "Women like silent men. They think they're listening." ' Following that, you simply need to welcome your new son-in-law and then propose a toast to 'The health and happiness of the bride and groom.'

SPEECH BY THE BRIDEGROOM AND BRIDE

It is increasingly popular, but not universal, for the bride to speak in addition to the bridegroom. If the bride does choose to speak, the content of her speech is usually similar to that of the bridegroom, and it is easy to divide the topics below between bride and groom. The speech is essentially a thank you to those who have made the day possible (biologically or financially) and a tribute to your new spouse. The order of the sections below is not particularly crucial. The speech is modelled on the bridegroom, rather than the bride, but the approach is easily adaptable.

I: Your new spouse and your new in-laws

Aim to mix genuine thanks with amusing stories. Use the questions below to trigger your own thoughts.

- *What do you need to thank them for?* Have they spent time and money on organising the event? Have they made you feel welcome as a son-in-law? Have they solved last-minute crises concerning the wedding? Have they given you bits of advice and tips (whether serious, humorous or even unintentional) that you have found useful?

- *What were your first impressions of the family?* Were you shaking with nerves before meeting them? Did her father grill you thoroughly about your intentions towards his daughter? Listen for the points that the bride's father makes in his speech about his first impressions of *you*, and see if there is any opportunity for banter or reanalysis of his thoughts.

- *How did you meet your wife?* Where were you? Were you nervous before the first date? Did you do anything odd to try and impress her? Did she do anything to try and impress you? Where did you used to go when you first started dating? What mutual hobbies or activities do you enjoy together?

- *What defines your wife?* What are her mannerisms? What nicknames do you have for her, and why? What annoying habits of yours has she changed? What do you love about her? How do you feel to be married to her? What are the moments you remember most – either happy ones or embarrassing ones?

II: Your parents

- *What do you need to thank them for?* Have they assisted with the wedding, either with money or hard work? Did they give you a good upbringing? Did they give you any advice before getting married – either explicitly or by example? Have they warmly welcomed the bride into the family?

- *What stories do you have about them?* Did they have any household rules as a kid that you always thought were strange? Do they have any peculiar characteristics – a funny walk, a strange laugh, an obsession with outdated music? What activities have they been involved in, either now or previously? What did they tell you off for when you were little? Did your family ever have a memorable holiday – for good reasons or bad?

III: *The assistants*

These might be a best man, bridesmaids, ushers, people who gave readings or acted as photographer/cameraman, people who helped with flowers and people who helped with the reception. Your sincere thanks might be accompanied by small gifts or perhaps just an anecdote or two.

- *What do you have to thank them for?* A word or two (but not an endless dedication) about how they've helped may be appreciated. Did they solve any minor crises either on the day or in the weeks before the wedding?
- *What's your best man like?* How do you know him? Did you have any worries about appointing him best man? Does he have any characteristics worth commenting on? Is he married himself – and would anyone be interested . . .? Do you have any great memories of pranks you two got up to together? (Although be careful in case he plans to use these stories in his speech as well.) Did he distinguish himself on the stag night at all?

IV: *Ending*

The ideal time to end is after you have thanked your assistants. The usual toast would be 'To the bridesmaids', with the best man rising next to reply on behalf of the bridesmaids. If the bride wishes to speak, however, the groom may offer a different toast, such as 'To my beautiful wife', leaving the bride to toast the bridesmaids.

SPEECH BY THE BEST MAN

By the time the best man rises to speak, most of the thanks will have already been given. (Though a sharp best man will be alert to anyone sitting with folded arms in the audience and looking indignant and unacknowledged.) Also, the audience will have probably been seated for some time listening to the other speeches. The best man's speech should therefore be a breath of fresh air – entertaining and responsive to the mood of the audience (which might mean last-minute editing if the audience is beginning to look restless). Since the bride's father and the groom have already talked about the bride, the best man's speech should focus primarily on the groom. It would, however, be a mistake not to pay *some* tributes to the bride – this is, after all, a wedding day and not the groom's birthday.

In addition, the best man's speech is formally a reply on behalf of the bridesmaids (who were toasted in the previous speech). It is easy to get carried away with pompous etiquette and some best men add endless dedications to the beauty of the bridesmaids. A simple statement like 'I agree, they look great' is fine. If you want to add more dedication then be wary of fawning.

I: The groom and bride as individuals

The main part of the speech will be stories and anecdotes about the groom, and to a lesser extent, the bride. The questions we must therefore ask are similar to those in the section about the speech given by the bride's father. It is a good idea to collect stories and tales from the groom's friends and family well in advance. Give them plenty of time to recollect, and then perhaps follow it up with a chat on the stag night. As we have suggested before, read the questions slowly and let them trigger your own thoughts.

- *Does the groom have any distinguishing mannerisms or character traits?* Does he have a goony smile or a funny stance? What do his parents say about his childhood – did he get into mischief, was he studious, did he have a burning desire for international rock stardom? What does his wife-to-be say his worst habits are? Does he have any moth-eaten jumpers or other shabby clothes that he loves to wear?
- *Does he have any hobbies or obsessions?* Does he have a fixation with a football team and a secret desire to play for them (if

only he had more talent)? What sort of music did he like as a kid, and how has it changed? Does he have a passion for his car? Does he admire his own driving skills, despite several speeding tickets and accidents? What does he do in his spare time – does he attend any classes or just lock himself in the garden shed?

- *What's his job?* Did he make any funny mistakes when he first started working there? Did he do anything noteworthy – such as getting promoted quickly, or passing some tough exams? What's he best at? What's he worst at?
- *What are your favourite stories about him?* What pranks did you used to get up to when you were younger? Did you used to take part in some activity together – a sports team, a school club or propping up the bar? Did anything happen on the stag night that is worth mentioning – a joke played on the groom or an argument with a nightclub bouncer?

II: The groom and bride as a couple

After talking about what sort of a guy the groom is, you can then describe how his life changed when he met his new wife.

- *How did they meet?* Where were you at this time? Did the groom (or bride) do anything silly to try and impress her (or him) in the early stages of their relationship? Where did they go on their first date? Have the venues for the dates become less impressive ever since, or more impressive?
- *How did he describe her at first?* What did he say to you before you first met her? Was he nervous about introducing her to his friends and family? Did she meet and surpass your expectations? What were your first impressions of her?
- *What mutual hobbies or activities do they have?* Do they play sport together and does one of them always win? Do they work in similar jobs – and do they understand each other's job?
- *What are they like as a couple?* What do people say about them? How have they changed since being together? Have

they corrected each other's little quirks, bad habits or dress sense?

III: Ending

You might want to end by saying a few words about what it means to you to be the groom's best man. Again, it is best not to fawn at this point, so mix your sentiments with the odd tale about nightmares you had, or horrible scenarios you envisaged.

The best man will normally then offer two toasts. The first toast may be 'To the bride and groom's future happiness', and the second to 'The host and hostess'. Sometimes, a third toast 'To absent friends' is also added. Unless someone else has been appointed to the task, the best man should then act as a compère for further events. So if the families decide they would like telegrams to be read or would like an open-mike session, then the best man should take charge of this. In addition, he should describe the programme for the rest of the evening.

4. SUMMARY

- **Don't worry, wedding speeches are easy.** You only need to speak for a short time, and yet you have a lifetime of material to use in your speech. The audience are merry, happy and want you to succeed.

- **Don't be a prisoner of etiquette.** The core etiquette is straightforward – the bride's father welcomes people and discusses the bride, the groom thanks people and the best man entertains people. We have recommended formats and toasts, but the details are entirely at the families' discretion.

- **Avoid getting into trouble.** Check the duties you are supposed to perform, such as who to thank and toast. Check the preferred names of the participants and their pronunciation. Check to see what subjects and topics are 'off limits'. Don't be jealous and don't drink too much.

- **The best material isn't in joke books, it's real stories about the people involved.** Ask the couple's friends for good stories about them and think about your favourite moments with them. Plan well in advance, and write down your thoughts. In general, aim for a short, unfawning speech about the bride and groom. Visual props can also add a kick to your performance.

- **Bride's father:** use the questions listed in the text as a prompt for anecdotes and stories about the bride. Do this well in advance of the wedding. Welcome the guests, talk about your daughter, welcome the groom into the family and toast the bride and groom.

- **Groom and bride:** use the questions listed in the text to spark off anecdotes and stories. Do this well in advance of the wedding. Thank the people who've made the wedding possible. Mix your thanks with friendly jibes and good-natured banter. End by toasting the bridesmaids.

- **Best man:** use the questions in the text to trigger anecdotes and stories. Do this well in advance, and follow it up by chatting to friends and family on the stag night (or earlier). Tell the audience what sort of a man the groom is; tell stories you have about him. Describe how his wife has changed his life. End by toasting the bride and groom and the host and hostess. Act as a compère for further events, such as an open-mike session (if necessary) or speeches by distinguished guests, and announce the programme for the rest of the evening.

GREAT SPEECHES IN HISTORY

PAUL OF TARSUS
WILLIAM PITT THE ELDER
SOJOURNER TRUTH
ABRAHAM LINCOLN
GEORGE GRAHAM VEST
WINSTON CHURCHILL
LOU GEHRIG
JAWAHARLAL NEHRU
RONALD REAGAN
JANE FONDA
GOUGH WHITLAM
STEVE BIKO
BILL CLINTON
DAVID TRIMBLE

GREAT SPEECHES IN HISTORY

Public speaking is an art, not a science. The best way to work out 'what works' is to look at what *has* worked. The speeches we have chosen, however, do not represent an 'official' list. They have been chosen with a number of considerations in mind. We have tried to include a range of speeches, from the political to the very personal, and a range of speakers, since great speakers are found in all walks of life. Two constraints have limited the representative character of the selection. Firstly, we have chosen a disproportionate number of modern speeches – not because they are better, but because, as teaching aids, they are more immediately *usable*. Secondly, we have, with the exception of one speech by the Apostle Paul, chosen speeches made in English. Few speeches work as well in translation as in their original tongue: the nuances of language are too easily lost.

There will, of course, be many who will wonder why their personal favourites have not been included: why no Lloyd George, no Gandhi, no Franklin D. Roosevelt, no Mandela? Had we included all those, of course, many more would be asking after others that were 'left out'. If readers wish that there had been more speeches at the end, we will have done our job well.*

Paul of Tarsus
Speech to the Areopagus[1]
Athens, c. 50 AD

Paul was a very committed evangelist for Christianity. He was also very canny. By speaking in cultural hubs like Athens, he ensured that

---

*Those in search of more great speeches may want to consult the appendix on further reading on page 255, especially pp. 258–259.

the message he preached would be spread far across the world. From what we know about his travels in Troas and Corinth, we know that Paul, more renowned for his letters, wasn't the most naturally gifted of speakers. Despite this, Paul addressed an enormous range of people in a wide range of different cultures. Paul presented this particular speech in Athens, in front of the Areopagus – an academic think-tank full of people from a wide range of backgrounds and with a diverse range of views. The speech would have found common ground with its diverse and multicultural audience and was, no doubt, spoken with the very real passion of a man who had travelled far, and in fear of death, to say what he believed.

Men of Athens! I see that in every way you are very religious. For as I walked around and looked carefully at your objects of worship, I even found an altar with this inscription: TO AN UNKNOWN GOD. Now what you worship as something unknown I am going to proclaim to you.

The God who made the world and everything in it is the Lord of heaven and earth and does not live in temples built by hands. And he is not served by human hands, as if he needed anything, because he himself gives all men life and breath and everything else. From one man he made every nation of men, that they should inhabit the whole earth; and he determined the times set for them and the exact places where they should live. God did this so that men would seek him and perhaps reach out for him and find him, though he is not far from each one of us. 'For in him we live and move and have our being.' As some of your own poets have said, 'We are his offspring.'

Therefore since we are God's offspring, we should not think that the divine being is like gold or silver or stone – an image made by man's design and skill. In the past God overlooked such ignorance, but now he commands all people everywhere to repent. For he has set a day when he will judge the world with justice by the man he has appointed. He has given proof of this to all men by raising him from the dead.

It is worth noting that the line 'In him we live and move' is a quote from the Cretan poet Epimenides. Legend has it that Epimenides was the person who advised the Athenians to erect altars to 'unknown gods'. The beauty of this speech is that Paul deals with the simple topic of idolatry very clearly, but also, in the last two sentences, provides just enough explanation of his deeper beliefs to entice the members of the Areopagus to hear more.

William Pitt the Elder
'Being a Young Man'[2]
London, 27 January 1741

In a parliamentary debate, Prime Minister Robert Walpole attempted to brush off his critic, William Pitt, with a dismissive remark about his age. This was Pitt's response:

Sir; the atrocious crime of 'being a young man', which the honourable gentleman has with such spirit and decency charged upon me, I shall neither attempt to palliate, nor deny, but content myself with wishing that I may be one of those whose follies may cease with their youth, and not one of that number who are ignorant in spite of experience. Whether youth can be imputed to any man as a reproach I will not, Sir, assume the province of determining; but surely age may become justly contemptible, if the opportunities which it brings have passed away without improvement, and vice appears to prevail when the passions have subsided. The wretch that, after having seen the consequences of a thousand errors, continues still to blunder, and whose age has only added obstinacy to stupidity is surely the object of either abhorrence or contempt, and deserves not that his grey head should secure him from insults. Much more, Sir, is he to be abhorred who, as he has advanced in age, has receded from virtue and becomes more wicked with less temptation; who prostitutes himself for money which he cannot enjoy and spends the remains of his life in the ruin of his country.

But youth, Sir, is not my only crime. I have been accused of acting a theatrical part. A theatrical part may either imply some peculiarity of gesture or a dissimulation of my real sentiments and an adoption of the opinions and language of another man. In the first sense, Sir, the charge is too trifling to be confuted and deserves only to be mentioned, that it may be despised. I am at liberty, like every other man, to use my own language; and though I may perhaps have some ambition to please this gentleman, I shall not lay myself under any restraints nor very solicitously copy his diction or his mien – however matured by age or modelled by experience. If any man shall, by charging me with theatrical behaviour, imply that I utter any sentiments but my own, I shall treat him as a calumniator and a villain; nor shall any protection shelter him from the treatment he deserves. I shall on such an occasion trample without scruple upon all those forms with which wealth and dignity entrench themselves. Nor shall anything but age restrain my resentment; age, which always brings one privilege – that of being insolent and supercilious without punishment.

But with regard, Sir, to those whom I have offended, I am of opinion that if I had acted a borrowed part I should have avoided their censure. The heat that offended them is the ardour of conviction and that zeal for the service of my country that neither hope nor fear shall influence me to suppress. I will not sit unconcerned while my liberty is invaded, nor look in silence upon public robbery. I will exert my endeavours at whatever hazard to repel the aggressor, and drag the thief to justice – whoever may protect him in their villainy, and whoever may partake of their plunder.

Pitt's is a classic 'destructive' speech. Leaping on the comment about his age, Pitt outwitted Walpole and used the careless remark as a stick with which to beat him. Anyone whose age has ever prevented them from being taken seriously will feel an inner cheer as they hear Pitt's forceful and passionate speech.

Sojourner Truth
'Ain't I a Woman?'[3]
Akron, 29 May 1851

Sojourner Truth was a former slave who became a radical social campaigner. This speech, given at a women's rights convention in Akron, Ohio, 1851, is still a battle cry for feminists today. To get an image of how the speech came across, imagine the crowd roaring their approval each time she asks 'ain't I a woman?'. Her short sentences provided ample opportunity for the crowd to interrupt with applause. And they did.

Well, children, where there is so much racket there must be something out of kilter. I think that 'twixt the negroes of the South and the women at the North, all talking about rights, the white men will be in a fix pretty soon. But what's all this here talking about?

That man over there says that women need to be helped into carriages, and lifted over ditches, and to have the best place everywhere. Nobody ever helps me into carriages, or over mud-puddles, or gives me any best place! And ain't I a woman?

Look at me! Look at my arm! I have ploughed and planted, and gathered into barns, and no man could head me! And ain't I a woman? I could work as much and eat as much as a man – when I could get it – and bear the lash as well! And ain't I a woman? I have borne thirteen children, and seen most all sold off to slavery, and when I cried out with my mother's grief, none but Jesus heard me! And ain't I a woman?

That little man in black there, he says women can't have as much rights as men, 'cause Christ wasn't a woman! Where did your Christ come from? From God and a woman! *Man* had nothing to do with Him.

If the first woman God ever made was strong enough to turn the world upside down all alone, these women together ought to be able to turn it back, and get it right side up again! And now they is asking to do it, the men better let them.

Obliged to you for hearing me, and now old Sojourner ain't got nothing more to say.

Sojourner Truth's speech fights prejudice with common sense, demolishing the notion of women's 'incapacity' with everyday examples, uncomplicated arguments and a powerfully self-confident style. It breaks all the arbitrary rules of grammar and vocabulary that some public speaking theorists blindly cling to, but follows all the principles of effective, audience-centred speaking (see pp. 54–58). Sojourner Truth speaks to her audience in terms they can relate to, and uses evidence that, unlike statistics, can easily be seen to be true. She turns incorrect interpretations of Christian morality on their head, but does not challenge that morality itself and so hits the audience's 'argumentative baseline' (see p. 55).

Abraham Lincoln
The Gettysburg Address
Gettysburg, 19 November 1863

The Battle of Gettysburg had humble beginnings. The town was rumoured to have an excess of shoes, which were in short supply during the American Civil War, and that was enough to prompt the opposing camps to battle there. This speech also had humble beginnings. The main oration at the commemoration ceremony for the soldiers killed at Gettysburg was given by Edward Everett – who was then considered the greatest orator of the day. President Lincoln was called upon merely to make some 'dedicatory remarks' at the Gettysburg cemetery. In just 269 words, Lincoln delivered one of the most famous – and one of the greatest – speeches ever.

Fellow countrymen. Four score and seven years ago, our fathers brought forth on this continent a new nation, conceived in liberty and dedicated to the proposition that all men are created equal.

Now we are engaged in a great civil war, testing whether that nation – or any nation so conceived and so dedicated – can long endure. We are met on a great battlefield of that war. We have come to dedicate a portion of that field as a final resting-place for those who here gave their lives that that nation might live. It is altogether fit and proper that we should do this.

But, in a larger sense, we cannot dedicate, we cannot consecrate, we cannot hallow this ground. The brave men, living and dead, who struggled here have consecrated it far above our poor power to add or detract. The world will little note nor long remember what we say here, but it can never forget what they did here. It is for us, the living, rather, to be dedicated here to the unfinished work which they who fought here have thus far so nobly advanced. It is rather for us to be here dedicated to the great task remaining before us: that from these honoured dead we take increased devotion to that cause for which they gave the last full measure of devotion; that we here highly resolve that these dead shall not have died in vain; that this nation, under God, shall have a new birth of freedom – and that government of the people, by the people, for the people shall not perish from the earth.

George Graham Vest
About a Dog
Missouri, 23 September 1870

George Graham Vest was a lawyer and, later, a US senator. The speech below was given in court as the summation of the case of a client who had taken someone to court for killing his dog – a case that Vest won.

Gentlemen of the Jury: The best friend a man has in the world may turn against him and become his enemy. His son or daughter that he has reared with loving care may prove ungrateful. Those who are nearest and dearest to us, those whom we trust with our happiness and our good name may become traitors to their faith. The money that a man has, he may lose. It flies away from him, perhaps when he needs it most. A man's reputation may be sacrificed in a moment of ill-considered action. The people who are prone to fall on their knees to do us honour when success is with us, may be the first to throw the stone of malice when failure settles its cloud upon our heads.

The one absolutely unselfish friend that man can have in this selfish world, the one that never deserts him, the one that never proves ungrateful or treacherous is his dog. A man's dog stands by him in prosperity and in poverty, in health and in sickness. He will sleep on the cold ground, where the wintry winds blow and the snow drives fiercely, if only he may be near his master's side. He will kiss the hand that has no food to offer. He will lick the wounds and sores that come in encounters with the roughness of the world. He guards the sleep of his pauper master as if he were a prince. When all other friends desert, he remains. When riches take wings, and reputation falls to pieces, he is as constant in his love as the sun in its journey through the heavens.

If fortune drives the master forth, an outcast in the world, friendless and homeless, the faithful dog asks no higher privilege than that of accompanying him, to guard him against danger, to fight against his enemies. And when the last scene of all comes, and death takes his master in its embrace and his body is laid away in the cold ground, no matter if all other friends pursue their way, there by the graveside will the noble dog be found, his head between his paws, his eyes sad, but open in alert watchfulness, faithful and true even in death.

This is hardly an ideal courtroom speech, but is a very good model for speeches given in a less confrontational environment. His words work not by persuading us of anything new, but by evoking images and sentiments that we already have. The feelings that come to the fore are not the speaker's, but our own. It is this that makes it so easy to identify with the speech. Which dog were you thinking of as you read it?

Winston Churchill
'A Total and Unmitigated Defeat'[4]
London, 5 October 1938

No collection of great speeches can miss out 'a Churchill'. When praised for his role in leading Britain through the Second World War, he said, 'I was not the lion. I just supplied the roar.' Churchill's wartime speeches are quoted so often, that many forget the weighty speeches he made before the war, particularly those which ominously warned of the impending threat. This speech was given in a debate in the House of Commons on a motion concerning the Government's policy of appeasement. Churchill rose to speak at ten past five. He was forceful, full of foresight and brutally honest.

Having thus fortified myself by the example of others, I will proceed to emulate them. I will, therefore, begin by saying the most unpopular and most unwelcome thing. I will begin by saying what everybody would like to ignore or forget but which must nevertheless be stated: namely that we have sustained a total and unmitigated defeat – and that France has suffered even more than we have . . .

[*Lady Astor*: Nonsense.]

When the Noble Lady cries 'nonsense', she could not have heard the Chancellor of the Exchequer admit in his illuminating and comprehensive speech just now that Herr Hitler had gained in this particular leap forward in substance all that he set out to gain . . .

Many people, no doubt, honestly believe that they are only giving away the interests of Czechoslovakia, whereas I fear we shall find that we have deeply compromised, and perhaps fatally endangered, the safety and even the independence of Great

Britain and France. This is not merely a question of giving up the German colonies, as I am sure we shall be asked to do. Nor is it a question only of losing influence in Europe. It goes far deeper than that. You have to consider the character of the Nazi movement and the rule which it implies. The Prime Minister desires to see cordial relations between this country and Germany. There is no difficulty at all in having cordial relations with the German people. Our hearts go out to them ... but there can never be friendship between the British democracy and the Nazi power – that power which spurns Christian ethics, which cheers its onward course by a barbarous paganism, which vaunts the spirit of aggression and conquest, which derives strength and perverted pleasure from persecution, and uses – as we have seen – with pitiless brutality the threat of murderous force ...

I have been casting about to see how measures can be taken to protect us from this advance of the Nazi power, and to secure those forms of life which are so dear to us. What is the sole method that is open? The sole method that is open for us is to regain our old island independence by acquiring that supremacy in the air which we were promised; that security in our air defences which we were assured we had, and thus make ourselves an island once again. That, in all this grim outlook, shines out as the overwhelming fact. An effort at rearmament the like of which has not been seen ought to be made forthwith, and all the resources of this country and all its united strength should be bent to that task ...

I do not grudge our loyal, brave people who were ready to do their duty no matter what the cost; who never flinched under the strain of last week. I do not grudge them the natural, spontaneous outburst of joy and relief when they learned that the hard ordeal would no longer be required of them at the moment. But they should know the truth. They should know that there has been gross neglect and deficiency in our defences. They should know that we have sustained a defeat without a war – the consequences of which will travel far with us along our road. They should know that we have passed an awful milestone in our history – when the whole equilibrium of Europe has been deranged, and that the terrible words have for the time being been pronounced against the Western democracies: 'Thou art weighed in the balance and found wanting.'

And do not suppose that this is the end. This is only the beginning of the reckoning. This is only the first sip, the first foretaste of a bitter cup which will be proffered to us this year unless by a supreme recovery of moral health and martial vigour, we arise again and take our stand for freedom as in the olden time.

This speech is full of substance. Churchill gives very definite policy proposals – such as the (now vindicated) need for superiority in the air. It is also a rhetorically canny speech – he turns what could be seen as an attack on ordinary people's naïvety into a cry against government misinformation. Churchill's skill is most evident in the way that he responds to Lady Astor and, in doing so, turns a speech by the Chancellor of the Exchequer into a speech against the government. Interruptions, when handled well, can provide a great boost to your speech. Incidentally, public speaking theorists might want to note, Churchill managed all of this with a lisp. Great speakers don't need to follow arbitrary rules of diction.

Lou Gehrig
'The Luckiest Man on the Face of the Earth'[5]
New York, 4 July 1939

Brilliant and universally popular, Lou Gehrig was one of America's greatest baseball players. In 1939 he was diagnosed with A.L.S., which causes spinal paralysis. His career, and his life, was to be brutally cut short. Addressing a 60,000-strong crowd at Yankee Stadium, he gave an inspiring speech that was rich with humility and grace. The secret behind the speech is that Gehrig just said, in a very down-to-earth way, what he really believed. Not only is this far easier than spending hours deliberately crafting the emotional content of your speech, it is also far more effective.

Fans, for the past two weeks you have been reading about a bad break I got. Yet today I consider myself the luckiest man on the face of the earth. I have been in ballparks for seventeen years and have never received anything but kindness and encouragement from you fans.

Look at these grand men. Which of you wouldn't consider it the highlight of his career to associate with them for even one day?

Sure, I'm lucky. Who wouldn't consider it an honour to have known Jacob Ruppert – also the builder of baseball's greatest empire, Ed Barrow – to have spent the next nine years with that wonderful little fellow Miller Huggins – then to have spent the next nine years with that outstanding leader, that smart student of psychology – the best manager in baseball today, Joe McCarthy!

Sure, I'm lucky. When the New York Giants, a team you would give your right arm to beat, and vice versa, sends you a gift, that's something! When everybody down to the grounds-keepers and those boys in white coats remember you with trophies, that's something.

When you have a wonderful mother-in-law who takes sides with you in squabbles against her own daughter, that's something. When you have a father and mother who work all their lives so that you can have an education and build your body, it's a blessing! When you have a wife who has been a tower of strength and shown more courage than you dreamed existed, that's the finest I know.

So I close in saying that I might have had a tough break – but I have an awful lot to live for.

Jawaharlal Nehru
On the death of Gandhi[6]
New Delhi, 2 February 1948

Mahatma Gandhi was the father of Indian independence and the embodiment of everything Indians had hoped their nation would become – tolerant, peaceful, and quietly spiritual. Instead, India suffered sectarian partition and a bloody war against Moslem Pakistan. Gandhi was on a fast for Moslem–Hindu reconciliation when he was assassinated by a Hindu extremist. The death of Gandhi felt to millions like the death of India's dream. In this speech to the Constituent Assembly, Indian Prime Minister Jawarhalal Nehru gave voice to the anguish of the nation and offered hope from the lessons of Gandhi's life.

A glory has departed and the sun that warmed and brightened our lives has set and we shiver in the cold and dark. Yet, he would not have us feel this way. After all, that glory that we saw for all these years, that man with the divine fire, changed us also – and such as we are, we have been moulded by him during these years; and out of that divine fire many of us also took a small spark which strengthened and made us work to some extent on the lines that he fashioned. And so if we praise him, our words seem rather small and if we praise him, to some extent we also praise ourselves. Great men and eminent men have monuments in bronze and marble set up for them, but this man of divine fire managed in his lifetime to become enshrined in millions and millions of hearts so that all of us became somewhat of the stuff that he was made of, though to an infinitely lesser degree. He spread out in this way all over India not in palaces only, or in select places or in assemblies but in every hamlet and hut of the lowly and those who suffer. He lives in the hearts of millions and he will be remembered for immemorial ages.

What can we say about him except to feel humble on this occasion? To praise him we are not worthy – to praise him whom we could not follow adequately and sufficiently. It is almost doing him an injustice just to pass him by with words when he demanded work and labour and sacrifice from us; in a large measure he made this country, during the last thirty years or more, attain to heights of sacrifice which in that particular domain have never been equalled elsewhere. He succeeded in that. Yet ultimately things happened which no doubt made him suffer tremendously – though his tender face never lost its smile and he never spoke a harsh word to anyone. Yet, he must have suffered – suffered for the failing of this generation whom he had trained, suffered because we went away from the path that he had shown us. And ultimately the hand of a child of his struck him down.

Long ages afterwards history will judge of this period that we have passed through. It will judge of the successes and the failures – we are too near it to be proper judges and to understand what has happened and what has not happened. All we know is that there was a glory and that it is no more; all we know is that for the moment there is darkness, not so dark certainly because when we look into our hearts we still find the living flame which he lighted there. And if those living flames exist, there will not be darkness in this land and we shall be able, with our effort, remembering him and following his path, to illumine this land again, small as we are, but still with the fire that he instilled into us.

He was perhaps the greatest symbol of the India of the past, and may I say, of the India of the future, that we could have had. We stand on the perilous edge of the present between that past and the future to be and we face all manner of perils and the greatest peril is sometimes the lack of faith which comes to us, the sense of frustration that comes to us, the sinking of the heart and of the spirit that comes to us when we see ideals go overboard, when we see the great things that we talked about pass into empty words and life taking a different course. Yet I do believe that perhaps this period will pass soon enough.

He has gone, and all over India there is a feeling of having been left desolate and forlorn. All of us sense that feeling, and I do not know when we shall be able to get rid of it, and yet together with that feeling there is also a feeling of proud thankfulness that it has been given to us of this generation to be associated with this mighty person. In ages to come, centuries and maybe millennia after us, people will think of this generation when this man of God trod on earth and will think of us who, however small, could also follow his path and tread the holy ground where his feet had been. Let us be worthy of him.

Perhaps the most important thing to note about this speech is the way in which Nehru acknowledged and sympathised with people's sense of anguish – and explained that he felt it too. This was a very humble speech. He was not lecturing the Indian people, he was giving voice to their shared pain. Note, for example, his use of the pronoun 'we': he never refers to his audience as 'you'. It is only because he acknowledged 'the darkness' that came with Gandhi's death that his audience listened when he reminded them that 'when we look into our hearts we still find the living flame which he lighted there'. The context of Nehru's speech was unique, but the lessons of it are not. Audiences need to feel that speakers understand them: speeches work best when you speak with the audience, not at them.

Ronald Reagan
'A Time for Choosing'[7]
27 October 1964

Ronald Reagan is one of the twentieth century's best speakers. Known as the 'Great Communicator', the former movie actor was a natural in front of the cameras. His arguments were simple, moralistic and easy to understand. He had little time for academic obscurantism, and no time for American self-criticism. His most beautiful speech is that given in honour of the Challenger Astronauts. His most controversial is the 'Evil Empire' speech. His most powerful and most impressive speech, 'A Time for Choosing', is reproduced here. Given as a televised address in support of then Republican Presidential candidate Barry Goldwater, it turns what could be seen as a dry economic agenda into a heartfelt defence of American values, and argues for individualist policies in terms of a collectivist rhetoric of national duty. Such ideas had been seen as reactionary and elitist since the 1929 Wall Street Crash destroyed President Hoover. This speech provided the rhetorical platform for their later re-emergence in much of the English-speaking world as radical and populist. Reagan's speech is a superb case study of how changing the rhetoric of the debate can transform the debate itself. (See the chapter on Language, pp. 89–109)

I am going to talk of controversial things. I make no apology for this.

It's time we asked ourselves if we still know the freedoms intended for us by the Founding Fathers. James Madison said, 'We base all our experiments on the capacity of mankind for self-government.'

This idea that government was beholden to the people, that it had no other source of power is still the newest, most unique idea in all the long history of man's relation to man. This is the issue of this election: whether we believe in our capacity for self-government or whether we abandon the American Revolution and confess that a little intellectual elite in a far-distant capital can plan our lives for us better than we can plan them ourselves.

The Founding Fathers knew a government can't control the economy without controlling people. And they knew when a government sets out to do that, it must use force and coercion to achieve its purpose. So we have come to a time for choosing.

Public servants say, always with the best of intentions, 'What greater service we could render if only we had a little more money and a little more power.' But the truth is that outside of its legitimate function, government does nothing as well or as economically as the private sector.

Yet any time you and I question the schemes of the do-gooders, we're denounced as being opposed to their humanitarian goals. It seems impossible to legitimately debate their solutions with the assumption that all of us share the desire to help the less fortunate. They tell us we're always 'against', never 'for' anything.

We are for a provision that destitution should not follow unemployment by reason of old age, and to that end we have accepted Social Security as a step toward meeting the problem. However, we are against those entrusted with this program when they practise deception regarding its fiscal shortcomings, when they charge that any criticism of the program means that we want to end payments.

We are for aiding our allies by sharing our material blessings with nations which share our fundamental beliefs, but we are against doling out money government to government, creating bureaucracy, if not socialism, all over the world.

We need true tax reform that will at least make a start toward restoring for our children the American Dream that wealth is denied to no one, that each individual has the right to fly as high as his strength and ability will take him . . . But we cannot have such reform while our tax policy is engineered by people who view the tax as a means of achieving changes in our social structure.

Have we the courage and the will to face up to the immorality and discrimination of the progressive tax, and demand a return to traditional proportionate taxation? Today in our country the tax collector's share is thirty-seven cents of every dollar earned. Freedom has never been so fragile, so close to slipping from our grasp.

Are you willing to spend time studying the issues, making yourself aware, and then conveying that information to family and friends? Will you resist the temptation to get a government handout for your community? Realise that the doctor's fight against socialised medicine is your fight. We can't socialise the doctors without socialising the patients. Recognise that government invasion of public power is eventually an assault upon your own business. If some among you fear taking a stand because you are afraid of reprisals from customers, clients, or even government, recognise that you are just feeding the crocodile hoping he'll eat you last.

If all of this seems like a great deal of trouble, think what's at stake. We are faced with the most evil enemy mankind has known in his long climb from the swamp to the stars. There can be no security anywhere in the free world if there is no fiscal and economic stability within the United States. Those who ask us to trade our freedom for the soup kitchen of the welfare state are architects of a policy of accommodation.

They say the world has become too complex for simple answers. They are wrong. There are no easy answers, but there are simple answers. We must have the courage to do what we know is morally right. Winston Churchill said that 'the destiny of man is not measured by material computation. When great forces are on the move in the world, we learn we are spirits – not animals.' And he said, 'There is something going on in time and space, and beyond time and space, which, whether we like it or not, spells duty.'

You and I have a rendezvous with destiny. We will preserve for our children this, the last best hope of man on earth, or we will sentence them to take the first step into a thousand years of darkness. If we fail, at least let our children and our children's children say of us we justified our brief moment here. We did all that could be done.

Jane Fonda
Broadcast to American Servicemen on Radio Hanoi[8]
North Vietnam, 22 August 1972

The Vietnam War divided Americans more than any conflict since the Civil War. One side saw it as an honourable and essential war against communism, others called it colonialism. In this broadcast, Jane Fonda goes behind the ideological tit-for-tat to discuss, in human terms, what war really does to people. She doesn't attack US servicemen – but appeals to them to abandon their support for 'Nixon's war'. She paints a picture that guides us to think not of generals and politicians but of ordinary people possessing extraordinary fortitude and warmth. This speech is full of passion but without aggression, is anti-militaristic without being unpatriotic, and appeals to people's compassion rather than to their politics. It is an ideal case study in how to humanise an argument.

This is Jane Fonda. During my two-week visit in the Democratic Republic of Vietnam, I've had the opportunity to visit a great many places and speak to a large number of people from all walks of life – workers, peasants, students, artists and dancers, historians, journalists, film actresses, soldiers, militia girls, members of the women's union, writers.

I visited the Dam Xuac agricultural co-op, where the silk worms are also raised and thread is made. I visited a textile factory, a kindergarten in Hanoi. The beautiful Temple of Literature was where I saw traditional dances and heard songs of resistance. I also saw an unforgettable ballet about the guerrillas training bees in the south to attack enemy soldiers. The bees were danced by women, and they did their job well.

In the shadow of the Temple of Literature I saw Vietnamese actors and actresses perform the second act of Arthur Miller's play *All My Sons*, and this was very moving to me – the fact that artists here are translating and performing American plays while US imperialists are bombing their country.

I cherish the memory of the blushing militia girls on the roof of their factory, encouraging one of their sisters as she sang a song praising the blue sky of Vietnam – these women, who are so gentle and poetic, whose voices are so beautiful, but who, when American planes are bombing their city, become such good fighters.

I cherish the way a farmer evacuated from Hanoi, without hesitation, offered me – an American – their best individual bomb shelter while US bombs fell near by. The daughter and I, in fact, shared the shelter wrapped in each other's arms, cheek against cheek. It was on the road back from Nam Dinh, where I had witnessed the systematic destruction of civilian targets – schools, hospitals, pagodas, the factories, houses, and the dike system. And, like the young Vietnamese woman I held in my arms clinging to me tightly, I thought, this is a war against Vietnam perhaps, but the tragedy is America's.

One thing that I have learned beyond a shadow of a doubt since I've been in this country is that Nixon will never be able to break the spirit of these people; he'll never be able to turn Vietnam, north and south, into a neo-colony of the United States by bombing, by invading, by attacking in any way. One has only to go into the countryside and listen to the peasants describe the lives they led before the revolution to understand why every bomb that is dropped only strengthens their determination to resist.

I've spoken to many peasants who talked about the days when their parents had to sell themselves to landlords as virtual slaves, when there were very few schools and much illiteracy, inadequate medical care, when they were not masters of their own lives.

But now, despite the bombs, these people own their own land, build their own schools, illiteracy is being wiped out, there is no more prostitution as there was during the time when this was a French colony. In other words, the people have taken power into their own hands, and they are controlling their own lives.

And after 4,000 years of struggling against nature and foreign invaders – and the last twenty-five years, prior to the revolution, of struggling against French colonialism – I don't think that the people of Vietnam are about to compromise in any way, shape or form about the freedom and independence of their country, and I think Richard Nixon would do well to read Vietnamese history, particularly their poetry, and particularly the poetry written by Ho Chi Minh.

Gough Whitlam
'Maintain Your Rage'[9]
Canberra, 11 November 1975

Many countries have constitutional conventions. It is a convention in Britain, for example, that the Queen never employs her powers to block legislation. The Australian people believed that the same conventions applied to their Governor-general – who, as the Queen's official representative in Australia, acts as the Head of State. In 1975, however, the Governor-general, Sir John Kerr, broke with convention by dismissing the elected Prime Minister, Gough Whitlam. Kerr then called on Malcolm Fraser, the Opposition leader in the House of Representatives, to form a government – even though Fraser's party had only a minority of seats in the House. The Proclamation of the Dissolution of Parliament was read from the steps of Parliament on a warm Australian summer evening. The Governor-general's official secretary read the proclamation, and ended with the traditional flourish: 'God save the Queen'. Whitlam responded . . .

Well may we say 'God save the Queen' because nothing will save the Governor-general. The proclamation which you have just heard read by the Governor-general's official secretary was countersigned 'Malcolm Fraser', who will undoubtedly go down in Australian history from Rememberance Day 1975 as 'Kerr's cur'.

They won't silence the outskirts of Parliament House, even if the inside has been silenced for the next few weeks.

The Governor-general's proclamation was signed after he had already made an appointment to meet the Speaker at a quarter to five. The House of Representatives had requested the Speaker to give the Governor-general its decision that Mr Fraser did not have the confidence of the House and that the Governor-general should call me to form the Government.

Maintain your rage and enthusiasm through the campaign for the election now to be held and until polling day.

If this speech demonstrates one thing, it is that great speeches – even those on momentous occasions – do not need to be long. It is also a factual speech – there is no waffle and padding. It wasn't enough to win Whitlam the election, but it is still an inspiration to Australian Republicans.

Steve Biko
On Democracy[10]
Pretoria, May 1976

Steve Biko was the unofficial leader of the Black Consciousness Movement of South Africa. Giving evidence in a trial of representatives of the South African Students Organisation, Biko was questioned in considerable detail about his political beliefs. In the exchange reproduced below, Biko was asked by the judge to defend his support for One Person One Vote.

Judge: But democracy is really only a success if the people who have the right to vote can intelligently and honestly apply a vote?

Biko: Yes, My Lord, this is why in Swaziland for instance where they have people sometimes who may not read the names of the candidates, they use signs.

Judge: Yes, but do they know enough of the affairs of the government to be able to influence it by a vote? I mean surely you must know what you are voting for, what you are voting about? Assuming now they vote on a particular policy, such as foreign investment, now what does a peasant know about foreign investment?

Biko: I think, My Lord, in a government where democracy is allowed to work, one of the principles that are normally entrenched is a feedback system, a discussion in other words between those who formulate policy and those who must perceive, accept or reject policy. In other words there must be a system of political education and this does not necessarily go with literacy. I mean Africa has always governed its peoples in the form of various chiefs, Chaka and so on, who couldn't write.

Judge: Yes, but the government is much more sophisticated and specialised now than in those days.

Biko: And there may be ways of explaining it to the people. People can hear, they may not be able to read and write, but they can hear and they can understand the issues when they are put to them.

Judge: Well take the Gold Standard, if we have to debate whether this government should go on the Gold Standard or go off the Gold Standard, do you think you know enough about it that the Government should be based on that vote?

Biko: Yes, I think I have a right to be consulted by my government on any issues. If I don't understand it, I may give over to someone else that I have faith in to explain it to me.

Judge: Well how can you? I mean that is your vote, and what about the ten other people who have votes?

Biko: The same applies to everybody else, and this is why we have the political process whereby things are explained. The average man in Britain does not understand the advantages or disadvantages of Britain becoming involved in the whole economic market, but when it becomes an issue for referendum, political organisers go out to explain and canvass their points of view, and the man in the middle listens to several people and decides to use what he has, the vote.

Great speeches don't have to be monologues. In fact, speeches often work better when there is interaction. Biko's court performance was so effective because he showed that he could take on the judge and win the argument. Biko's aim was not to convince the apartheid-constrained court to bring an acquittal but to convince black South Africans to keep up the struggle. Weeks later, schoolchildren began an uprising. As Biko's biographers put it, 'courage is infectious'.

Bill Clinton

'I Did Have a Relationship
(But it's Time to Move On)'[11]
Washington DC, 17 August 1998

US President Bill Clinton gave this speech, on television, after admitting to a grand jury investigation that he had had a relationship with a former White House intern, a fact which he had previously seemed to deny. The admission (and the evidence that provoked the admission) led Independent Counsel investigator, Ken Starr, to accuse the President of perjury. Clinton used this speech to appeal over the heads of the senators, who would conduct his trial, to the American public. He needed to (1) avoid incriminating himself; (2) show remorse to a public who felt let down and (3) get people to leave this issue behind and focus on more positive aspects of his Presidency. His speech helped to achieve all three by (1) sticking to this legal defence that he had not broken the law; (2) admitting and apologising for personal wrongdoing and (3) depicting the investigation as a partisan distraction from the real problems of the American people. The speech is so skilfully crafted that we have chosen to add commentary to point out how each line – each word – serves his purpose.

Good evening.
[Short introduction, none of the usual Clinton folksiness: he knows his audience are impatient and angry.]

This afternoon in this room, from this chair, I testified before the Office of Independent Counsel and the grand jury.
[He is implying that the choice of background for the broadcast was incidental, and not – as it almost certainly was – selected after much discussion with PR consultants on what would convey the most calm image in such turbulent times.]

I answered their questions truthfully, including questions about my private life, questions no American citizen would ever want to answer.
[There are two messages here. The surface one is a constitutional/ philosophical point about the right to privacy. The second one, hinted at but not spelt out, is that all of us have sinned, and should be careful of throwing stones.]

Still, I must take complete responsibility for all my actions, both public and private.
[Implication: the affair and his evasions of admission are private matters, not public ones.]

And that is why I am speaking to you tonight.
[He flatters us – we, the public, are the ultimate judges of the President.]

As you know, in a deposition in January, I was asked questions about my relationship with Monica Lewinsky. While my answers were legally accurate, I did not volunteer information.
[This is the legal defence.]

Indeed, I did have a relationship with Ms Lewinsky that was not appropriate. In fact, it was wrong. It constituted a critical lapse in judgement and a personal failure on my part for which I am solely and completely responsible.

[*This is the most brilliant part of the speech. He begins 'I did have a relationship with Ms Lewinsky', which sounds like a reversal of the previous claims that he did not. But the sentence goes on: '. . . that was not appropriate.' He does not, therefore, contradict his prior claim that there was no 'sexual' relationship. He is only admitting an inappropriate one. The public get the moral confession they need in order to forgive him; the investigators don't get the legal confession they need to win a prosecution. His follow-up line – 'in fact, it was wrong' – confirms this strategy of admitting (unspecified) personal mistakes, but not indictable offences.*]

But I told the grand jury today and I say to you now that at no time did I ask anyone to lie, to hide or destroy evidence or to take any other unlawful action.

[*The legal defence again, and a line demarcating personal issues from public ones.*]

I know that my public comments and my silence about this matter gave a false impression. I misled people, including even my wife. I deeply regret that.

[*Clinton's admission that he misled 'even' his wife sounds like a profound* mea culpa, *with the penitent man actually drawing attention to his sins. But he knows that in legal terms the more serious crime is misleading a court, and in political terms the more serious crime is misleading the public. He is drawing attention away from these by confessing to something irrelevant to his opponents' case.*]

I can only tell you I was motivated by many factors. First, by a desire to protect myself from the embarrassment of my own conduct.

[*He admits the selfish motive first, allowing him to get on to more advantageous points. If he'd first tried to claim more principled motivations, we wouldn't have believed him. He had to disarm our suspicions first.*]

I was also very concerned about protecting my family. The fact that these questions were being asked in a politically inspired lawsuit, which has since been dismissed, was a consideration, too. In addition, I had real and serious concerns about an independent counsel investigation that began with private business dealings twenty years ago – dealings, I might add, about which an independent federal agency found no evidence of any wrongdoing by me or my wife over two years ago. The independent counsel investigation moved on to my staff and friends, then into my private life. And now the investigation itself is under investigation. This has gone on too long, cost too much and hurt too many innocent people.

[*He discredits the investigation, and casts the investigation, not his affair, as the cause of all the damage done to people.*]

Now, this matter is between me, the two people I love most – my wife and our daughter – and our God.

[*Clinton the family man, Clinton the moralist.*]

I must put it right, and I am prepared to do whatever it takes to do so.

[*'Don't think you have to impeach me in order for me to suffer because of this.'*]

Nothing is more important to me personally. But it is private, and I intend to reclaim my family life for my family. It's nobody's business but ours.

[*Once the confessions are over and done with, he gets tough, but not on his own behalf (which would look selfish) but on behalf of his family, which legitimises his righteous anger.*]

Even presidents have private lives. It is time to stop the pursuit of personal destruction and the prying into private lives and get on with our national life. Our country has been distracted by this matter for too long, and I take my responsibility for my part in all of this. That is all I can do. Now it is time – in fact, it is past time – to move on. We have important work to do – real opportunities to seize, real problems to solve, real security matters to face. And so tonight, I ask you to turn away from the spectacle of the past seven months, to repair the fabric of our national discourse, and to return our attention to all the challenges and all the promise of the next American century.
[*The investigation is harming America, harming you the viewer. Time to move on.*]

Thank you for watching. And good night.
[*Simple, polite, confident ending to a superb speech. Game, Set and Match to Clinton.*]

David Trimble
'Looking for Peace Within the
Realms of the Possible'[12]
(Nobel Lecture)
Oslo, 10 December 1998

David Trimble is leader of the 'pro-British' Ulster Unionists, Northern Ireland's biggest political party. On Good Friday 1998 he signed a wide-ranging agreement with his former enemies, for which he was awarded the Nobel Peace Prize. Observers of his Nobel Lecture expected either hopeful waffle (the politician stereotype) or fierce ranting (the Unionist stereotype). What they got instead was an exceptionally rigorous and insightful analysis of the dangers of romanticism. It is a model 'intelligent speech' – well structured, well argued and well presented. The speech is sophisticated without being complicated, intellectual without being pretentious, critical without being cynical. If you think that the most effective speeches never really say anything, this speech might just change your mind.

Your Majesties, Members of the Norwegian Nobel Committee, Excellencies, Ladies and Gentlemen.

The Nobel Prize for peace normally goes to named persons. This year the persons named are John Hume and myself, two politicians from Northern Ireland. And I am honoured, as John Hume is honoured, that my name should be so singled out.

If you want to hear of a *possible* Northern Ireland, not a Utopia, but a normal and decent society, flawed as human beings are flawed, fair as human beings are fair, then I hope not to disappoint you.

Some suggest that I might explicate at some little length, like a peace scientist, on any lessons learnt in the little laboratory of Northern Ireland.

I have, in fact, some fairly serious reservations about the merits of using any conflict – not least Northern Ireland – as a model for the study, never mind the solution, of other conflicts.

In fact if anything, the opposite is true. Let me spell this out.

I believe that a sense of the unique, specific and concrete circumstances of any situation is the first indispensable step to solving the problems posed by that situation.

Now, I wish I could say that that insight was my own. But that insight into the central role of concrete and specific circumstance is the bedrock of the political thought of a man who is universally recognised as one of the most eminent philosophers of practical politics. I refer, of course, to the eminent eighteenth-century Irish political philosopher and brilliant British Parliamentarian, Edmund Burke.

He was the most powerful and prophetic political intellect of that century. He anticipated and welcomed the American revolution. He anticipated the dark side of the French revolution. He delved deep into the roots of that political violence, based on the false notion of the perfectibility of man, which has plagued us since the French revolution.

Burke is the best model for what might be called politicians of the possible: politicians who seek to make a working peace, not in some perfect world, that never was, but in this, the flawed world, which is our only workshop.

Because he is the philosopher of practical politics, not of visionary vapours, because his beliefs correspond to empirical experience, he may be a good general guide to the practical politics of peacemaking.

Burke was particularly acute about the problems of dealing with revolutionary violence – that political, religious and racial terrorism that comes from the pursuit of abstract virtue, the urge to make men perfect against their will.

Amos Oz has also arrived at the same conclusion. Recently in a radio programme he was asked to define a political fanatic. He did so as follows, 'A political fanatic,' he said, 'is someone who is more interested in you than in himself.' At first that might seem as an altruist, but look closer and you will see the terrorist. A political fanatic is not someone who wants to perfect himself. No, he wants to perfect you. He wants to perfect you personally, to perfect you politically, to perfect you religiously, or racially, or geographically. He wants you to change your mind, your government, your borders. He may not be able to change your race, so he will eliminate you from the perfect equation in his mind by eliminating you from the earth.

'The Jacobins,' said Burke, 'had little time for the imperfect.'

We in Northern Ireland are not free from taint. We have a few fanatics who dream of forcing the Ulster British people into a Utopian Irish state, more ideologically Irish than its own inhabitants actually want. We also have fanatics who dream of permanently suppressing northern nationalists in a state more supposedly British than its inhabitants actually want.

But a few fanatics are not a fundamental problem. No, the problem arises if political fanatics bury themselves within a morally legitimate political movement. Then there is a double danger. The first is that we might dismiss legitimate claims for reform because of the barbarism of terrorist groups bent on revolution.

In that situation experience would suggest that the best way forward is for democrats to carry out what the Irish writer, Eoghan Harris, calls 'acts of good authority' – that is, acts addressed to their own side.

Thus each reformist group has a moral obligation to deal with its own fanatics. The Serbian democrats must take on the Serbian fascists. The PLO must take on Hammas. In Northern Ireland, constitutional Nationalists must take on Republican dissident terrorists and constitutional Unionists must confront Protestant terrorists.

There is a second danger. Sometimes in our search for a solution, we go into denial about the darker side of the fanatic, the darker side of human nature. Not all may agree, but we cannot ignore the existence of evil. Particularly that form of political evil that wants to perfect a person, a border at any cost.

It has many faces. Some look suspiciously like the leaders of the Serbian forces wanted for massacres such as that at Srebenice, some like those wielding absolute power in Baghdad, some like those wanted for the Omagh bombing.

Here we come again to Burke's belief that politics proceeds not by some abstract notions or by simple appeal to the past, but by close attention to the concrete detail and circumstance of the current specific situation.

'Circumstances,' says Burke, 'give in reality to every political principle, its distinguishing colour, and discriminating effect. The circumstances are what render every civil and political scheme beneficial or noxious to mankind.'

That is the nub of the matter. True I am sure of other conflicts. Previous precedents must not blind negotiators to the current circumstances. This first step away from abstraction and towards reality, should be followed by giving space for the possibilities for progress to develop. What I have looked for is a peace within the realms of the possible. We could only have started from where we actually were, not from where we would have liked to be.

And we have started. And we will go on. Sometimes we will stumble, maybe even go back a bit. But this need not matter if in the spirit of an old Irish proverb we say to ourselves, 'Tomorrow is another day'.

What we democratic politicians want in Northern Ireland is not some utopian society but a normal society. The best way to secure that normalcy is the tried and trusted method of parliamentary democracy. So the Northern Ireland Assembly is the primary institutional instrument for the development of a normal society in Northern Ireland.

Like any parliament, it needs to be more than a cockpit for competing victimisations. Burke said it best, 'Parliament is not a congress of ambassadors from different and hostile interests; which interests each must maintain, as an agent and an advocate, against other agents and advocates; but Parliament is a deliberative assembly of one nation, with one interest, that of the whole; where not local purposes, nor local prejudices ought to guide, but the general good resulting from the general reason of the whole.'

Some critics complain that I lack 'the vision thing'. But vision in its pure meaning is clear sight. That does not mean I have no dreams. I do. But I try to have them at night. By day I am satisfied if I can see the furthest limit of what is possible. Politics can be likened to driving at night over unfamiliar hills and mountains. Close attention must be paid to what the beam can reach and the next bend.

Both communities must leave [sectarianism] behind, because both created it. Each thought it had good reason to fear the other. As Namier says, the irrational is not necessarily unreasonable. Ulster Unionists, fearful of being isolated on the island, built a solid house, but it was a cold house for Catholics. And

Northern Nationalists, although they had a roof over their heads, seemed to us as if they meant to burn the house down.

None of us are entirely innocent. But thanks to our strong sense of civil society, thanks to our religious recognition that none of us are perfect, thanks to the thousands of people from both sides who made countless acts of good authority, thanks to a tradition of parliamentary democracy which meant that paramilitarism never displaced politics, thanks to all these specific, concrete circumstances we, thank God, stopped short of that abyss that engulfed Bosnia, Kosovo, Somalia and Rwanda.

Thank you for this prize for peace. We have a peace of sorts in Northern Ireland. But it is still something of an armed peace. It may seem strange that we receive the reward of a race run while the race is still not quite finished. But the paramilitaries are finished. Politics is not finished. It is the bedrock to which all societies return. Because we are the only agents of change who accept man as he is and not as someone else wants him to be.

There are two traditions in Northern Ireland. There are two main religious denominations. But there is only one true moral denomination. And it wants peace.

I am happy and honoured to accept this prize on behalf of all the people of Northern Ireland.

I am happy and honoured to accept the prize on behalf of all the peacemakers from throughout the British Isles and farther afield who made the Belfast Agreement that Good Friday at Stormont.

They did good work that day.

And tomorrow is now another day.

Thank you.

The key ways in which Trimble made his speech so easy to follow are his clear theme and his clear structure. Note how all the arguments – even the jokes – fit in with the theme: you remember very clearly at the end that ideological politics is dangerous, even if you can't remember the detail. Perhaps the most important lesson of this speech, however, is that speeches don't have to be vapid. Reading this speech, you probably found yourself thinking less about the rhetorical twists than about the argument that was being made – one definite sign of a truly effective speech.

APPENDIX 1: BRAINWASHING, TRICKERY AND FREE SPEECH

This book is about how to become a great public speaker. It is not a book about morality. Yet whenever we give public speaking workshops, we are always asked about the morality of public speaking and persuasion. An American student once asked one of us whether he felt it was immoral to teach a skill that has so often been misused. (The perceptive student was, incidentally, a keen member of his local gun club.) The author replied that he thought the same about free speech as Churchill thought about democracy – that it's a terrible system, but that every alternative is much worse. But what about teaching people how to lie, how to 'brainwash', how to fool the public?

That isn't what we teach, of course, and that isn't what this book is about. The book is, however, about persuasive speaking – and persuasive speaking isn't always used for good. So is it right to teach it? Brian MacArthur, author of the superb *Twentieth Century Speeches*, attempted to fend off such charges by arguing that 'most of the speeches [in his book] demonstrate the power of oratory for good rather than evil. They articulate dreams, offer hope, stir hearts and minds, and offer their audiences visions of a better world.'[1] This is an old line of defence, based on one by Aristotle in his classic *Rhetoric*: oratory itself is neutral, he argued, it is people's underlying purpose that makes it moral or immoral.[2] The problem with this type of justification, however, is that each side just ends up swapping examples to prove their point: 'I've found another nasty speech'; 'I've found another nice one.' There is, however, a more pressing moral case: freedom.

The right to argue one's case is one of the pillars of any free society, a principle reflected in people's mistrust of censorship and in people's support for adversarial legal systems and multi-party democracies. If, however, only a tiny elite have sufficient *ability* to argue a case, then the right to free speech is effectively infringed.

This book is an attempt to spread the knowledge currently available only to a small elite to a much wider, self-selecting rather than pre-selected, audience. Society will be a lot fairer – and a lot safer – if as many people as possible can participate effectively in public debate and discussion. This book won't change the world, but further restrictions on free speech *would*: they would make it much worse.

APPENDIX 2: DEBATING AT THE OXFORD UNION

The Oxford Union was founded in 1823, and has been the world's most respected and most exciting debating forum ever since. British Prime Ministers who were officers of the Oxford Union include Salisbury, Gladstone, Asquith, Macmillan and Heath. Nobel Peace Prize Winners who have spoken at the Oxford Union include Yasser Arafat and Shimon Peres; David Trimble and John Hume; Desmond Tutu and F. W. de Klerk; Mother Teresa and the Dalai Lama. Sinn Fein leader Gerry Adams spoke at the Union at a time when the British Government still banned his voice from television. Malcolm X came to speak at a time when the American political establishment regarded him as a dangerous enemy of the state. The Oxford Union's insistence on standing up for free speech has at times led to great controversy. It has also made for electrifying debates.

The style of debate at the Oxford Union is engaging, entertaining and, occasionally, brutal. Guest speakers debate alongside Oxford students on issues ranging from international politics to personal relations, and everything in between. Though warmly welcomed at a pre-debate reception (partly to loosen their tongues before going into the debating chamber), famous guests get no special treatment in the debate itself. Many have been surprised at the tough questioning they receive from students who they expected to be awe-struck and deferential. Perhaps more surprisingly, guests usually find the whole experience rather refreshing, and are virtually always glad to be invited back again.

THE FORMAT OF THE DEBATES
All debates take place in the Union debating chamber – a building modelled on the chamber of the House of Commons.

The debaters sit on opposite sides of the house – the 'proposition speakers' on the right-hand side of the President, and the 'opposition speakers' on the left-hand side. The President is the co-ordinating figure in the debate.* Although all debaters will have about ten minutes in which to present their case, the President can cut them short (if they are causing offence) or allow them to carry on (if the audience is in awe). Extensions and cuts are, however, rare as they act against a sense of fair play.

The debate begins with a speech for the proposition, which defines the grounds of the argument and sets out the case that will be argued. So, for example, if the motion was 'This House believes that European integration is not in the interests of the people of Europe', the first speaker would clarify *exactly what grounds* the debate is based on, such as whether it will focus on monetary union or political union or both. A clear definition of the grounds of the debate serves to ensure that all debaters argue the same issue. There's no point, for example, in all the proposition speakers arguing the merits of monetary union if all the opposition speakers focus on political union. That would not be a debate – it would just be a series of speeches.

The first speaker for the opposition follows immediately, and is expected to respond to and rebut the main arguments of the proposition, rather than merely reading from a pre-prepared script. The debate then alternates between the remaining speakers for the proposition and the opposition.

There are usually between three and five debaters on each side. Each has a different role. Those who speak early tend to set out the grounds of the debate and present the main arguments. Those who speak later tend to sum up and clarify the main issues of the debate.

---

*To avoid confusion, we will refer to 'The President' when discussing the person who chairs the debate. When we refer to 'the speaker', we do not mean 'Speaker' in the parliamentary sense (i.e. the person who chairs the debate), but merely the debater who happens to be addressing the audience at any one instant.

After the final speeches there is a floor debate, where members of the audience have an opportunity to speak. Audience members signal to the President, who selects speakers in the cyclic order: speeches in proposition of the motion, speeches in opposition, speeches in abstention, speeches in proposition . . . and so on. When the President senses that the debate is drawing to an end, he will call on two speakers – one from the proposition benches and one from the opposition benches, to conclude the debate. In summing up, good speakers pay careful attention to inconsistencies, contradictions and abandoned arguments in their opponents' speeches – in other words, the idea is to make your own side's arguments seem appealing and the other side's arguments seem simplistic and flawed.

As in the British House of Commons, audience members then vote by leaving through a door marked either 'aye' or 'no'. Discussion continues in the bar.

RULES TO ENSURE FAIR PLAY

The 'rules' of debate are much less rigid than are often imagined: don't go over time, don't be too offensive, and don't attack your own side. In a competition debate the procedures are tightened up, but they still don't dictate what arguments and style to adopt. Formalities and procedures are important, but they are there to support, rather than hold back, powerful argument and effective presentation.

Apart from the format of the debate, the only 'rules' are those that govern interruptions to speeches. Throughout, audience members or other speakers may offer 'points of information' (short questions or comments) to the debater who is addressing the audience. To do this, they merely need to stand up and say 'Point of Information'. The debater then may choose to listen to the point, or decline it, or postpone it till later – and will signal this to the person who offered the point. Whilst it is sensible not to accept every point that is offered, speakers who refuse all such requests quickly lose the support of the audience. (See pages 130 to 131 for more on points of information.)

Very rarely, a debater or an audience member may show such disregard for the other participants in the debate – perhaps by being grossly offensive or speaking out of turn – that somebody feels the need to ask the President to intervene. If such a situation arises, the proper procedure is to stand up and say, to the President, 'Point of Order'. The President will then halt the debate to listen to the point. A point of order is, therefore, a big disruption and should only be used to prompt a President who has let the debate get out of control.

Debating at the Oxford Union is not so much about 'club rules': it's about learning how to win people over and about learning how to be won over yourself.* The precise details of the debate – such as the length of the speeches and the number of debaters on each side – are entirely flexible. A debate is just a fair way of having an argument.

---

*Readers wanting to know more about the Oxford Union and debating can visit the Oxford Union website at: < http://www.oxford-union.org >

APPENDIX 3: CONFIDENCE-BUILDING EXERCISES AND GAMES

In this book we have tried to lay out the key principles of effective public speaking. We began by asking you to throw away artificial 'rules' of public speaking and concentrate instead on winning over your audience. The theme, structure, content and language of your speech should all be geared towards this purpose – as, of course, should your style of presentation. Some types of public speaking require specialist skills – in particular, speaking to the media, speaking at business meetings and speaking at weddings. The core principle, however, remains the same: don't look at public speaking from the point of view of the person speaking, look at it from the point of view of the people listening. All the speeches given in the Great Speeches section were so effective for precisely this reason. For this reason, too, we have decided to recap the lessons of the book not by reprinting the chapter summaries but through a series of games.

These are designed to improve confidence and proficiency in public speaking. They are also intended to be fun, and are a bit like playing charades. They have been successfully used to train speakers of all standards in many different countries. The underlying goal is to provide a bridge between conversation (a form of speaking which most people find easy) and public speaking (a form of conversation most people find difficult). Specifically, the games will help you to:

- Eliminate fear of public speaking.
- Speak more naturally.
- Revise key tips that were given in the earlier parts of the book.

The games work best when there are between four and twenty participants (although there is nothing to stop you trying them in a group of two, or even on your own in front of a mirror). A group of this size provides an ideal audience to practise in front of – large enough to create an atmosphere, but not so big as to be intimidating. Many people therefore find it easy to improve their confidence and natural style by speaking in front of small groups.

Anyone can benefit from these games. Schoolteachers may want to use versions of them to run public speaking courses at their schools and families can play them with the future in-laws as a way of practising for the wedding speeches.

Five games are suggested below. They each come with a set of tips on the most common faults that people make when playing them.

EXERCISE 1: WARM-UP

Aim: This short game serves to get people ready for the other exercises, as well as giving people an opportunity to say hello and get acquainted.

Game: Very simple. Start with the person holding this book. Stand up and just say one interesting fact – only one sentence long. Then sit down again. The person on your left should do the same, and so on until everyone has spoken. If playing with strangers, you may want everyone to stand up and just say their name, and therefore just use this exercise as a means of introduction.

Lesson: Even this simple warm-up exercise illustrates two common mistakes that people make:

1. *They didn't speak loudly enough.* Speak loudly to grab the audience's attention. Speak louder than you think you need to. Audiences do not struggle to hear a whispering speaker.

2. *They had poor eye contact with the audience.* Eye contact is deeply personal, and keeps the audience alert. It is hard to drift off to sleep when you know the speaker will be looking directly at you. If you don't believe that people respond to eye contact, try sitting on a train and staring at the stranger opposite.

EXERCISE 2: CLASH

Aim: This game gets people used to speaking in a natural manner in front of the group. It also helps people who need to respond to others' speeches – such as people involved in panel discussions or debates, or even those who want to make an after-dinner reply speech. The ability to respond to unexpected events and think quickly are the hallmarks of a great public speaker.

Game: Split the group into two straight lines facing each other, and pair everyone off with the person opposite. The people on the left-hand side of the room each speak for about half a minute or so on one of the subjects below. (It is best if all the speakers choose a different subject.) After all the people on the left-hand side have spoken, those on the right-hand side try to contradict, disagree and find fault with their opponent's speech. Nobody needs to speak for longer than one minute. Everyone is welcome to use notes – as long as they don't read them verbatim. Then repeat the game with left and right sides switched over. Suggested topics for people to talk about are:

1. My favourite advert is . . .
2. If I ruled the world . . .
3. Older people make better lovers because . . .
4. If I could go back to school . . .
5. Yesterday, all my troubles seemed . . .
6. I'd never get married because . . .
7. The strangest thing about my family is . . .

8. I'm finally facing my Waterloo . . .
9. This Government is actually quite good . . .
10. I hate political correctness because . . .
11. My most embarrassing moment was . . .
12. My spouse's strangest mannerism is . . .
13. I'd never live in Britain because . . .
14. I hate my job because . . .
15. Nobody loves me . . .
16. I wish they could all be Californian . . .
17. I'm proud of our football team . . .
18. Modern music is *just such* a noise . . .
19. My favourite toy as a kid was . . .
20. Censorship laws are too harsh . . .
21. Beware of . . .
22. What I hate most is . . .

More experienced speakers may want to develop this game. Take a newspaper and use the headlines as topics to speak about. More serious topics will require you to speak slightly longer – but try to limit speeches to just a few minutes each, or the game will tend to drag on.

Lesson: This simple exercise will hone your rebuttal skills very quickly. It is also a gentle introduction for those who are not used to speaking in public. The main points to watch and evaluate are:

1. *Use notes but don't read.* Using brief notes helps to keep you on track. Reading word-for-word kills your style and makes spontaneity impossible.
2. *Be natural.* You don't have to put on an act as you speak. You are not an eighteenth-century political statesman, so you don't need to use phrases like 'It is my most respectful submission that . . .' unless you do actually speak like that normally. Your style and words should be 'you'.

3. *Rebuttal is focussed on the opponent's words.* Those on the right-hand side (who *replied* to the speeches) need to take on board the opponent's argument and then destroy it. For instance, if a speaker says, 'The strangest thing about my family is my kids' friends . . .' it is much better *argumentative* technique to rebut their speech by arguing that their children's friends are nice, rather than to propose something different such as 'No, the strangest thing about your family is your dress sense.'

4. *Rebuttal is often effective if you 'theme' the opposition.* Characterising the opposition is an effective way to turn an audience against them. Is there an easy compartment you can put them in? For instance, if your opponent argued 'Yesterday, there was discipline in schools, but not any more', then it would be easy to characterise them as some kind of self-appointed and out-of-touch colonel who believes that children should be given a-firm-thrashing-and-it-never-did-me-any-harm. You can have great fun describing the characteristics of such a stereotype. If done sensitively you can make your opponent's words seem less enticing.

5. *Voice and eyes.* Have you heeded the advice of the warm-up game? Look at your audience. Speak so they can all hear you.

EXERCISE 3: THE INTELLECTUAL OUTLAW

Aim: We discussed the Intellectual Outlaw technique on pages 30 to 36. We saw that it can be used to rebuff a popular opponent. Here we will practise advocating unpopular causes. Defending the indefensible is a good way to sharpen your public speaking skills, as it requires tone of voice and language to be used very carefully.

Game: Everyone speaks for a minute or so in defence of an unpopular cause. It is best if you choose your own subjects for this, and the greater their relevance to those playing, the better. If you are stuck for ideas, here are some sample subjects:

'Imperialism and colonialism were good'
'Nudity and indecency laws should be abolished'
'Castro was the best thing that ever happened to Cuba'
'It was a good move when Caligula made his horse a Senator'
'There are some benefits to child labour'
'Son, it's a good idea if you drop out of college and play the guitar for a living'

It is often a good idea to question each speaker for a minute or so after the speech. The more mainstream and gentle the speaker is in real life, the more comic (or impressive) it is to see them speak in defence of unorthodox views.

Lesson: Fighting a popular *status quo* viewpoint is a hard test for a public speaker, so the speeches you made in this game were perhaps the hardest you will ever make. There are some points to note, however:

1. *Did you 'admit' certain facts up front?* When pressing an unpopular case, you need to demonstrate to the audience that you are reasonable and balanced in your views. In order to build a bridge between your viewpoint and the audience's, it is best to admit certain facts. For example, 'I know the Cuban economy is in an appalling state, and I know that personal liberty is sometimes violated in Cuba. But I would argue that this is more to do with the economic embargo than it is with Castro's leadership . . .' In other words, show sympathy for the popular viewpoint, but demonstrate that it is irrelevant to the point you are making.

2. *Did you watch your style?* A tone of voice similar to a conspiracy theorist or a madman in a sandwich board will win you no converts. You need to sound reasonable, calm and understanding. Your subject matter is not agreeable to the audience, so you must be.

3. *Did you watch your language?* When 'admitting' to certain facts (see point 1), you must ensure that your language is forthright. You do not want to appear to be 'holding back' from self-criticism where necessary. Similarly, throughout the whole speech, you need to be careful of the resonances that your words have – 'Western conspiracy' sounds opinionated, but 'it is regrettable that this policy was adopted by the West' sounds as though you are merely commenting on facts.

4. *Was your style more natural during the question-and-answer session?* We see this regularly at the Oxford Union. A speaker will address the audience for twenty minutes or so, and then field questions. Commonly, the speaker is far more relaxed and natural during the question-and-answer sessions than during the main address. This kind of ease is what you should try to capture in your speech. Many speakers have tried this game in reverse, with the question-and-answer session first, in order to 'carry over' that natural style into the speech.

EXERCISE 4: CONTINUITY

Aim: This game will get you used to thinking on your feet. It will also demonstrate that many pre-speech nerves are completely unjustified.

Game: Form a circle. One player acts as a chairperson. The person on the left of the chairperson starts telling a story. After a few seconds, the chairperson claps their hands and the next person in the circle continues the story. Although each player only speaks for a few seconds, the players must try to remain as faithful as they can to the story. There is no point in one player saying 'Then, there was a knock at the door . . .' only to be followed by the next player continuing '. . . but she didn't answer it and instead went to Bermuda on holiday'. The game is often most fun if there's some banter with the chairperson, so having a lively chairperson who is prepared to take a bit of ridicule is essential.

Lesson: This is a tough exercise, which is why everyone speaks for only a few seconds. You cannot properly prepare your contribution, and you have to ad-lib. If you survived it then note these points:

1. *Humour is best when relevant.* The funniest moments in the game were probably not scripted jokes, but were lines thought up on the moment or things that happened as the game and story developed.
2. *Speakers get more nervous than they need to.* Your heart was probably pounding and your nerves greatest just before you spoke. But looking back, you were *too* nervous, weren't you? The task was much easier than your nerves lead you to believe. Remember this when you are faced with an easier task – such as speaking when preparation is allowed, unlike in a continuity game.

EXERCISE 5: ALIBI

Aim: This game is an old favourite of law students.[1] It is set in a courtroom and throws up many subtle issues to do with persuasion.

Game: A crime was committed last Saturday between 9 p.m. and 11 p.m. Two people ('the suspects') leave the room and have five minutes to concoct an alibi to explain where they were last Saturday evening. They return, one at a time, to be questioned by two 'prosecutors'. The prosecutors try to break down the suspects' alibi by asking unexpected questions and getting contradictory answers from the two suspects. After having questioned each suspect for a few minutes, the prosecutors sum up the suspects' responses and try to convince 'the jury' (i.e. everyone else in the room) that the suspects are guilty. The jury take a vote to decide.

Lesson: This game is, of course, very different from a real trial. The nerves are not 'real', and nor are the advocacy techniques. As a public speaking exercise, however, it throws up some interesting issues:

1. *Thinking on your feet.* In debates, committee meetings and question-and-answer sessions, public speakers are exposed to questions. Most people find it very hard to think on their feet when an audience is looking at them. The only way to avoid this is through practice. Keep playing this game in front of small informal groups of friends, and you will soon become used to thinking while others watch you.

2. *Subtleties of questioning.* On pages 162 to 166, we saw how the way you phrase a question can, to some extent, fix the answer you will get. For example, rapid-fire aggressive questioning might draw an unexpected admission from a hot-headed and over-confident suspect. Timid suspects might, however, be better when questioned gently in order to get them to talk more openly. Leaving long gaps after your questions might encourage nervous suspects to talk in order to fill up the embarrassing pauses. All of these are just suggestions – the important point is just that the style you adopt for questioning people or negotiating with people very much depends on who you are talking to (see pages 166 to 172).

3. *Finding flaws.* Contradictions are not always of the superficial type, such as where one suspect claims the alibi was a man and the other claims it was a woman. Instead, contradictions normally lie a little deeper, and, as outlined on pages 79–82, require the prosecutor to draw some logical inferences from the statements. Contradictions in the suspects' testimonies are not the only flaws that a prosecutor may find. There may

be unsupported assertions, errors of fact and so on. These concepts were all discussed more fully on pages 76 to 87.

4. *You're enjoying yourself.* When you bought this book you might well have thought that public speaking was a painful chore – unavoidable, of course, but painful. Now you're practising quite difficult public speaking exercises and you're having a good time. The techniques involved in 'ordinary' public speaking are much easier. And once you get into your stride, making a presentation to your board of directors, setting out the need for policy reform to a group of politicians, and, yes, even giving a speech at your best friend's wedding, can actually be enjoyable. Still difficult, of course, but no longer 'impossible', and sometimes even fun. Everyone can be a great public speaker.

REFERENCES

INTRODUCTION
1. C. Patten, *East and West*, Times Books, London, 1998.
2. See, for example, Adlai Stevenson introducing John F. Kennedy in 1960, quoted in B. Cochran, *Adlai Stevenson: patrician among the politicians*, Funk & Wagnalls, New York, 1969.
3. Quoted in 'Youngest Peer Steps Into The Limelight' *The Times*, 5 April 1995.

THE BASICS

THE BASICS OF SPEECH-BUILDING
1. R. Anholt, *Dazzle 'em with Style: The Art of Oral Scientific Presentation*, W. H. Freeman and Company, New York, 1994, p. 24.
2. See, for example, R. Bewes, *Speaking in Public – Effectively*, Christian Focus Publications, UK, 1998, p. 99.
3. See, for example, D. Carnegie, *How to Develop Self-Confidence and Influence People by Public Speaking*, Vermillion, London, 1998 (First Edition Cedar, USA, 1957), pp. 39–41.
4. See, for example, Jim Anderson, 'Documents cast a doubt on US claims in Pinochet case', *Bangkok Post*, 13 August 1999.
5. *Hansard*, 23 February, 1999, column 187.

THE BASICS OF PRESENTATION
1. Reproduced from *Yes, Prime Minister* by Jonathan Lynn and Antony Jay with permission of BBC Worldwide Limited. Copyright © Jonathan Lynn and Antony Jay.
2. K. Grahame, *Wind in the Willows*, Methuen, London, 1977 (First edition 1908), p. 248.
3. R. Reich, *Locked in the Cabinet*, Vintage, New York, 1998, pp. 37–38.
4. 'Remarks by the President to the People of Israel', White House Press Office, 13 December 1998.

5. M. K. Gandhi, *The Story of My Experiments with Truth*, Greenleaf, London, 1984.
6. British Airways *High Life Magazine*, September 1998.

BUILDING A SUCCESSFUL SPEECH

THEME

1. Tony Blair, at the 'What The Papers Say' awards, February 1997.
2. D. Carnegie, *How to Develop Self-confidence and Influence People by Public Speaking*, Vermillion, London, 1998 (First edition Cedar, USA, 1957), p. 215.
3. Ronald Reagan, 'Evil Empire', 8 March 1983. Taken from *Great Speeches*, HarperCollins audio books, London, 1997.
4. Tony Blair, speech to the Dail, 26 November 1998.
5. Richard Nixon, 'Checkers' speech, 1952.
6. George Canning, 'The Deliverance of Europe', 1798. Taken from *The Parliamentary History of England*, Vol. XXXIV AD 1798–1800, London. A more accessible source is *Great Speeches in History*, Naxos audio books, 1996.
7. See, for example, W. J. McGuire and D. Papageorgis, *Journal of Abnormal and Social Psychology*, **62**, 327 (1961); A. McAlister et al., *American Journal of Public Health*, **70**, 719 (1980) and R. Atkinson et al., *Introduction to Psychology*, 1990 (Harcourt Brace Jovanovich Inc., Orlando, Florida, 1990). These references, and others, describe both the initial research on inoculation and also its application to, for example, warning children about the dangers of smoking..
8. A. McAlister et al., ibid. and R. Atkinson et al., ibid.

STRUCTURE

1. Malcolm X quoted in *The World's Great Speeches*, ed. L. Copeland and L. Lamm, Dover Publications Inc., New York, 3rd edition, 1973, p. 825.
2. Susan B. Anthony quoted in *The Penguin Book of Historic Speeches*, ed. B. MacArthur, Penguin Books, London, 1996 (First edition Viking, 1995), p. 440.
3. For a good demonstration of this see, for example, P. Noonan, *On Speaking Well*, Regan Books, USA, 1999, pp. 18–20.

CONTENT

1. Aristotle, *Rhetoric*, Book II, 1395b, 5. Taken from *Great Books of the Western World*, (Encyclopaedia Britannica Inc. from Ross, W. D. (ed.) *The Works of Aristotle*, by arrangement with Oxford University Press).

2. 1 Corinthians 9: 19–22, NIV version.

3. Rev. Martin Luther King, Jr., 'I Have A Dream', taken from *Great Speeches*, HarperCollins Audio Books, London, 1997.

4. For extracts of speeches by Lloyd George, Lenin, William I and Sojourner Truth, see, for example, ed. B. MacArthur, *The Penguin Book of Historic Speeches*, Penguin Books, London, 1996 or *The World's Great Speeches*, ed. L. Copeland and L. Lamm, Dover Publications Inc., New York, 1973.

5. Lord Scarman, in *Davis v Johnson* [1979] AC 264.

6. B. MacArthur, *The Penguin Book of Historic Speeches*, Penguin Books, London, 1996, p. 222.

7. R. Clements, *A Sting in the Tale*, Inter-Varsity Press, UK, 1995, p. 7.

8. George Bernard Shaw quoted in L. Copeland and L. Lamm, *The World's Great Speeches*, p. 208.

9. Aristotle, *Rhetoric*, Book II, 1394a, 11, *op. cit.*

10. Quoted by Charles Francis in *How to Stop Boring Your Audience to Death*, New York Chapter of the International Association of Business Communicators in New York City, 16 January 1996.

11. P. Noonan, *On Speaking Well*, Regan Books, USA, 1999, p. 11.

12. Just one of many excellent one-liners that can be found in Bill Bryson's *Notes from a Small Island*, Corgi Audio Books, a division of Transworld Publishers, 1995.

13. Taken from Victor Lewis-Smith, *Inside the Magic Rectangle*, Indigo, 1996 (First edition Victor Gollancz, 1995). Many other excellent one-liners can be found in this book.

14. Taken from Darrel Huff, *How to Lie with Statistics*, Penguin Books, London, 1991 (First edition Victor Gollancz, 1954). This book provides the starting point for much advice offered in this chapter.

15. Taken from *Private Eye's Bumper Book of Boobs*, Private Eye Productions Ltd, London, 1990 (First edition 1973).

16. S. Fry and H. Laurie, *A Bit of Fry & Laurie*, p. 75.
17. General Douglas MacArthur, Farewell Address to Congress, 20 April 1951, taken from *Great Speeches*, HarperCollins Audio Books, 1997.
18. W. J. Clinton, Second Inaugural Address, 20 January 1997.
19. Tony Benn, Tribute to John Smith, House of Commons, 12 May 1994. Extract taken from *Great Speeches in Parliament 1989–1999*, Politico's Publishing, 1999.
20. This box is based on William Poundstone's excellent book, *Labyrinths of Reason*. Penguin Books, London, 1991 (First edition Anchor Books, USA, 1988).

LANGUAGE

1. Children and Young Person's Act 1933, s. 59.
2. D. Tannen, *That's Not What I Meant*, Virago, London, 1992.
3. D. Landes, *The Wealth and Poverty of Nations*, Norton, New York, 1999, p. 426.
4. P. Noonan, *On Speaking Well*, Regan Books, USA, 1999, p. 51.
5. S. E. Lucas, *The Art of Public Speaking*, McGraw-Hill, New York, 1989, p. 215.
6. L. Copeland and L. Lamm, *The World's Great Speeches*, Dover Publications Inc., New York, 1973, p. 208.
7. This is a paraphrased and simplified extract from a lecture by Ben White to the Institute of Social Studies, The Hague, September 1999. The actual correspondence between the ILO and its Bengali translators has never been published. Our version of events is an impressionistic 'best guess' at what was said, based on anecdotal reports. For a full explanation of the ILO distinction between 'child work' and 'child labour', see ILO, *World of Work*, Geneva, June 1993, pp. 6–7.
8. *Prime Minister's Address to the Nation: East Timor*, Office of the Prime Minister, Canberra, Australia, 19 September 1999.
9. Several of these examples – and more not mentioned here – are cited in O. Thomson, *Easily Led*, Sutton Publications, Gloucestershire, 1999, p. 49–52.
10. Ben White, *op.cit.*, September 1999.
11. This story is recounted in S. Pinker, *The Language Instinct*, Penguin, London, 1994, p. 389.

12. *The Economist*, 19 December 1998, p. 83.
13. R. Reich, *op.cit.*, p. 112.
14. *Newsweek*, 16 November 1998, p. 40.
15. G. Mikes, *How to be an Alien*, Penguin, London, 1966 (1946), p. 42. Reproduced by permission of Penguin Books Ltd.

PRESENTING A SUCCESSFUL SPEECH

EVENT MANAGEMENT

1. The details of the experiments described are given in S. Milgram, *Journal of Abnormal and Social Psychology*, 67, 371–378 and S. Milgram, *Obedience to Authority: An Experimental View*, New York: Harper&Row.
2. J. O'Farrell, *Things Can Only Get Better*, Transworld, London, 1998, p. 35.
3. D. Carnegie, *How to Stop Worrying and Start Living*, Vermillion, London, 1998 (First edition Cedar 1953).
4. O. Thomson, *op.cit.*

SPEAKING IN A TECHNOLOGICAL AGE

1. O. Thomson, *op.cit.*
2. P. Krugman, *Geography and Trade*, MIT, Cambridge, Mass., 1993, p. 54.

SPECIALIST SKILLS

SPEAKING THROUGH THE MEDIA

1. Safi, quoted in O. Thomson, *Easily Led*, p. 317.
2. P. Flynn, *Commons Knowledge: How to be a Backbencher*, Seren, London, 1997, p. 84.
3. See, for example, R. Bewes, *Speaking in Public – Effectively*, Christian Focus Publications, UK, 1998, p. 9.
4. See *The Times*, *Independent* and *Daily Telegraph*, 16 November 1990.
5. E. De Bono, *I am Right, You are Wrong*, Penguin, London, 1991, p. 267.
6. From an interview in *The L-word* – 'Swarthmore's Journal of progressive thought' – December 1997. Also < http://www.sccs.swarthmore.edu/org/lword/dec97/interview.html >.

7. M. Thatcher, *The Downing Street Years*, HarperCollins, New York, 1993, p. 626.
8. M. Thatcher in *Conservative Realism – New Essays in Conservatism*, ed. K. Minogue, HarperCollins, London, 1996, p. xiii.

SPEAKING IN BUSINESS AND COMMITTEE MEETINGS

1. More information about this mnemonic can be found in, for example, P. Forsyth, *30 Minutes . . . To Get Your Own Way*, Kogan Page (London), 1999, p. 20–21.
2. The idea for this example was taken from J. O'Connor and I. McDermott, *An Introduction to NLP*, ThorsonsAudio, 1996.
3. Again, for more on this concept, see J. O'Connor and I. McDermott, *ibid*.
4. J. Major, *John Major: The Autobiography*, HarperCollins, London, 1999, p. 209.

GREAT SPEECHES IN HISTORY

1. The Apostle Paul, quoted in Acts 17: 22–31, NIV version.
2. William Pitt the Elder, 'Being a Young Man', *Parliamentary History of England*, Vol. XII AD 1741–1743, London. A more accessible source is *Great Speeches in History*, Naxos Audio books, 1996.
3. Based on the records of Frances Gage, a delegate at the conference. Gage's version gives a 'phonetic' representation of Truth's accent.
4. Recorded in *Hansard*, 5 October 1938, 339 H.C. Deb. 5s. More accessible sources are B. MacArthur, *The Penguin Book of Twentieth-Century Speeches*, Penguin, London, 1993 (First edition Viking, London, 1992); and also from < http://www.winstonchurchill.org >.
5. Extracts taken from, e.g. < http://www.historyplace.com >.
6. This speech was given to the Constituent Assembly of India on 2 February 1948. It is printed in L. Copeland and L. Lamm, *The World's Great Speeches*, Dover Publications, Inc., New York, 1973, pp. 619–620.
7. Transcript of the television recording.
8. Transcript from the US Congress House Committee on Internal Security, Travel to Hostile Areas, HR 16742, 19–25 September, 1972, p. 7671.

9. Taken from E. Gough Whitlam, *The Truth of the Matter*, Penguin, London, 1979.

10. Extracts of the court reports from the SASO/BPC Trial can be found in S. Biko, *I Write What I Like*, Bowerdean, London, 1996 (1978).

11. From the Office of the Press Secretary, The White House, 17 August 1998.

12. D. Trimble, The Nobel Lecture, Oslo 10 December 1998.

APPENDIX 1: BRAINWASHING, TRICKERY AND FREE SPEECH

1. B. MacArthur ed., *The Penguin Book of Twentieth-Century Speeches*, Penguin, London, 1993 (First edition Viking, London, 1992), p. xvii.

2. Aristotle actually went further and claimed (without proof) that truthful arguments have a natural tendency to prevail over untruthful arguments.

APPENDIX 3: CONFIDENCE-BUILDING EXERCISES AND GAMES

1. This game is described in more detail, along with other similar games, in Glanville William's classic book *Learning the Law*, originally published by Stevens & Sons (London), 1945.

FURTHER READING

GENERAL PUBLIC SPEAKING TEXTS

Aristotle, Rhetoric, from *Great Books of the Western World*, Encyclopaedia Britannica Inc., reprinted from W. D. Ross (ed.) *The Works of Aristotle*, by arrangement with Oxford University Press.

This ancient text is rich in information and advice. However, Aristotle's work is not, obviously, a ready-reference practical public-speaking guide, as he is much more concerned with how rhetoric can be classified. However, this was a pioneering work, and its advice has permeated all public speaking texts since.

Peggy Noonan, *On Speaking Well*, Regan Books, USA, 1999.

Peggy Noonan wrote some of President Reagan and George Bush's best speeches and has great experience in non-political speechwriting as well. Her book is easily readable and is full of sound advice. Moreover, for tips on how to write speeches for others, her book is second to none.

Dale Carnegie, *How to Develop Self-confidence and Influence People by Public Speaking*, Vermillion, London, 1998 (Cedar, 1957), and also *The Quick and Easy Way to Effective Speaking*, Vermillion, London, 1998 (1962).

Two classic titles which are particularly good at inspiring and encouraging inexperienced speakers. Dale Carnegie uses an empirical approach – drawing on the advice of the great speakers of history – to discover the secrets of successful public speaking.

Greville Janner MP, *Janner's Complete Speechmaker*, Century, London, 1999 (Sixth edition).

Not modestly titled, but certainly accurately titled. The book contains not only advice on speechmaking, but also a selection of great speeches (curiously weighted in favour of the author's parliamentary colleagues) and a compendium of quotes and anecdotes. Particularly good for speakers concerned with their appearance in front of the media.

Chris Steward and Mike Wilkinson, *Bluff Your Way in Public Speaking*, Ravette Books, Sussex, 1998.

At just sixty pages, it's short, easy to read and a good introduction to the subject. The only question is: why did it need two people to write it?

Stephen Lucas, *The Art of Public Speaking*, McGraw-Hill, New York, 1989.

A comprehensive series of lessons for students at high school or university. A very usable guide, if a touch rigid.

SPECIALIST PUBLIC SPEAKING TEXTS

Richard Bewes, *Speaking in Public – Effectively*, Christian Focus Publications, 1998.

This author is a vastly experienced preacher. This book sets out both his advice on public speaking, and also his beliefs on how preachers should approach the subject. Richard Bewes is the minister of All Souls, a busy church in the centre of London, and anyone wanting to actually hear an example of a model sermon should visit http://www.allsouls.org and buy a copy of their tape entitled 'Dead and Buried' (cat. number: E001/43a) (a talk delivered by Rico Tice on 3 October 1999).

Robert Anholt, *Dazzle 'em with Style: The Art of Oral Scientific Presentation*, W. H. Freeman and Company, New York, 1994.

One of only a few books on how to give scientific presentations. The basic skills of public speaking are no different for scientists, but some might prefer this 'niche' book. The advice it offers is wholly sound, but the technical language might be off-putting to the larger niche of people-who-aren't-biochemists.

Michael Billig, *Arguing and Thinking: A Rhetorical Approach to Social Psychology*, Cambridge University Press, Cambridge, 1996.

A comprehensive and well-written book on rhetoric, psychology and people's attempts to learn about oratory. If you liked the introduction to our book, then this book will also appeal.

Patrick Forsyth, *30 Minutes to Get Your Own Way*, Kogan Page Ltd, London, 1999.

A short, pocket-sized introduction on how to communicate persuasively.

Sonya Hamlin, *How to Talk So People Listen: What Works, What Doesn't and Why*, Thorsons, London, 1993 (First edition Harper & Row, New York, 1988).

The author of this work is a chat show host and runs a communications consultancy. The book is concerned with persuasive communication, rather than public speaking *per se*, and contains some sound advice. Packed full of bullet points and snazzy management-speak, it is probably reaching out to sharply dressed businesspeople rather than poetic orators, students or people who are generally relaxed about life.

Trevor Sather (ed.), *Pros and Cons: A Debater's Handbook*, Routledge, London, 1999 (eighteenth edition).

The best resource book for debating that is currently available. The book gives a brief introduction to debating and then contains speech material, facts and arguments to use when debating various current affairs issues. See also the associated website, set up by the editor of the book: http://www.britishdebate.com. The website contains many guides and tips on debating, including an excellent guide to logical argument called 'Dan Neidle's Guide To Debating', which is written by a top London lawyer.

Paul Flynn MP, *Commons Knowledge: How to be a Backbencher*, Seren, Bridgend, 1997.

A witty and informative guide for political speakers and those who have frequent dealings with the media.

Theodore Zeldin, *Conversation: How Talk Can Change Your Life*, Harrill Press, London, 1999.

Pocket-sized, seventy pages long and full of nice ideas about, touchingly, 'how to make the world a better place'. Worth a read.

Deborah Tannen, *That's Not What I Meant*, Virago, London, 1992.

Not a public speaking guide but a book on conversation. Many of the lessons, however, apply to public speaking too.

Steven Pinker, *The Language Instinct*, Penguin, London, 1994.

An entertaining and insightful book that will be enjoyed by anyone with an interest in how language works.

MULTIMEDIA COLLECTIONS OF FAMOUS SPEECHES

Brian MacArthur (ed.), *The Penguin Book of Historic Speeches*, Penguin, London, 1996, and *The Penguin Book of Twentieth-Century Speeches*, Penguin, London, 1993.

Two wonderful and comprehensive collections of great historical speeches. The speeches aren't discussed or analysed (except to set the scene of the speech), and so the book is devoted to faithfully reproducing the texts of the speeches. Ideal reading for anyone who enjoyed reading the 'Great Speeches in History' section of our book.

Lewis Copeland and Lawrence Lamm (eds.), *The World's Great Speeches*, Dover Publications Inc., New York, 1973.

Another massive compilation of speeches. Although not updated since 1972, the book contains speeches from every other era. It contains a number of informal speeches, and thus makes an ideal complement to MacArthur's books.

Owen Collins, *Speeches that Changed the World*, HarperCollins Publishers, London, 1998.

Again, another fine compilation of speeches. Particularly strong on speeches by literary figures such as Dickens and Whitman.

http://www.historyplace.com/speeches

A great website, full of famous and not-so-famous speeches. Regularly updated, with a 'speech of the week' section and a listing of important speeches.

Great Speeches, HarperCollins Audio Books, London, 1997.

Contains five-minute snippets of famous speeches. With one exception, all speeches are made by American political (or socio-political) figures – so it is not an entirely balanced selection. Nonetheless, the editing is very good, and the snippets are authentic recordings of the politicians themselves.

Great Political Speeches, Compiled by Peter Hill, for Hodder Headline Audio Books, London, 1996.

These are somewhat shorter extracts of speeches. All speeches are by British politicians, but the diversity within that field is immense. The tape starts with an authentic recording of Prime Minister Gladstone speaking in 1889 and ends with a speech at a party conference in 1995. The chronological ordering of the speeches means that the tape provides a fascinating history of Britain's last 100 years.

Great Speeches in History, Naxos Audio Books Ltd, 1996.

This is more of a 'classical' selection of great speeches. Speeches by Socrates, Oliver Cromwell, and Lincoln aren't, obviously, authentic recordings. This does tend to take some of the thrill out of listening, but the selection of speeches is interesting and the actors' readings of the speeches are generally very good.

Great Speeches in Parliament 1989–1999, Politico's Publishing, 1999.

A good selection of speeches from Britain's first ten years of televised Parliamentary debates. There is a discerning mix of lighthearted, serious, sad and aggressive speeches. What is striking, however, is just how bad some politicians are at public speaking. As we said right at the start of the book, great speakers aren't only found in parliament.

INDEX OF FAMOUS SPEAKERS

Entries marked with an asterisk (*) can be found in the 'Great Speeches' section.

ABOUT THE AUTHORS

Dominic Hughes was formerly a scholar of Jesus College, Oxford and holds a doctorate in Physical Chemistry. He has trained a wide range of people in the UK and abroad in debating and public speaking. He currently works in the law and lives happily in London.

Benedict Phillips (formerly New College, Oxford and later Huygens Scholar at the Institute of Social Studies, the Hague) has led advocacy and campaigns for a number of top non-government organisations, worked in the House of Commons and trained people from across the world in effective communication. He currently works for the international development organisation Oxfam.

Benedict and Dominic are one of the Oxford Union's most successful pair of debaters in recent years. They were finalists in the XVIII World Universities Debating Championships and have won other national and international debating tournaments.